Praise for *Desert Priestess:*

"Anne Key has told a great story about her time in the Nevada desert as a modern-day priestess of the ancient Egyptian Goddess Sekhmet; it is raw and expressive and so interesting. I loved it!"
— **Vicki Noble**
The Double Goddess: Women Sharing Power and
The Motherpeace Tarot

"... a sincere road map for those, like her, who sincerely seek a feminine divine response to contemporary U.S. society, politics, and established religions."
— **Ana Castillo**
Goddess of the Americas/La Diosa de las Américas
and *The Guardians*

"We live in a time in which increasing numbers of authentic spiritual seekers are leaving our mainstream religions in droves... *Desert Priestess* reveals the shape of this new tradition as we turn within ourselves to discover our connections with the transpersonal forces that have been waiting for us to recognize them and to invite them into our lives once again. A compelling read!"
— **Hank Wesselman, PhD**
The Spiritwalker Trilogy, Awakening to the
Spirit World (with Sandra Ingerman) and
The Bowl of Light: Ancestral Wisdom from a Hawaiian Shaman

"Filled with candor, astonishing philosophical insights, and kaleidoscopic accounts of the primal and uncompromising beauty of the Nevada desert, *Desert Priestess* offers readers an invitation to experience our own belonging as women. In its grounded wisdom, humility, and compassion, this memoir reminds readers of the beauty of living a life connected to the life forces of this earth."

— **Cristina Eisenberg**
Conservation biologist, mythology scholar, and author,
The Wolf's Tooth: Keystone Predators, Trophic Cascades,
and Biodiversity

"… a book about what it really means to be a practicing priestess in the present day… This an honest account of Anne's three-year journey… and the nature of priestessing a modern-day goddess temple … Read this book to be inspired as a priestess yourself."

— **Kathy Jones**
Priestess of Avalon in Glastonbury, England, and founder of the
Glastonbury Goddess Temple; author,
Priestess of Avalon: Priestess of the Goddess

"… a moving account of a personal confrontation with the mythology of the Goddess Sekhmet of ancient Egypt … as relevant today as ever."

— **Larry Dossey, MD**
The Power of Premonitions, Healing Words,
and Reinventing Medicine

"... shines and sparkles with her deep wisdom, her humility, and her growing understanding and awareness of an ancient spirituality experienced and manifested in the early twenty-first century... A book for all of us—whatever our spiritual path."

— **Cheryl Straffon**
Editor, *Goddess Alive*, and author *Pagan Cornwall: Land of the Goddess, the Earth Goddess,* and *Daughters of the Earth*

Desert Priestess:
a memoir

Anne Key

Goddess Ink, Ltd.
Las Vegas

Printed in the United States of America.

ISBN: 978-0-9833466-0-9

Published by
Goddess Ink, Ltd.
8470 Helena Ave.
Las Vegas, NV 89129
www.goddess-ink.com

Designed by Soujanya Rao
Front cover photograph by Candace Peace Ross
Back cover photograph by John Hardham
Author photograph by Ian Flude
All artwork by Katlyn Breene (www.mermadearts.com)

To Kalli Rose
Her Star illuminates my path

CONTENTS

Introduction xi

A Temple in the Desert 1

Sekhmet in Her Desert Temple • *My First Day and Night at the Temple* • *The Temple at the Crux* • *Sekhmet* • *First Month* • *"I Am Black"* • *My First Public Ritual*

Daily Life of a Twenty-First-Century Priestess 23

Typical Day • *Animal, Vegetable, Mineral Offerings*

The Folk 34

Visitors to the Temple: The Random and the Not Well Intentioned • *Making the Circle* • *Clarity and Open-Hearted Generosity* • *Journeys: Healers and Warriors* • *Women and the Goddess Temple* • *Men and the Goddess Temple* • *Priestesses: On Creating the Circle of Sisters* • *Feeling Alone in the Circle*

Initiation and Personal Evolution 60

The Parameters of Mind and Profession • *Initiation: The Severing of the Head* • *Initiation: The Demarcation*

CONTENTS

Spinning the Wheel: The Rituals of the Year 68

The Seasonal Dance of Light and Dark • Full Moon Meanings • The Priestess Readies for Ritual • Rituals: Full Moon Release • Rituals: The First Day of Spring • Rituals: The First Day of Summer • Rituals: Mid-Autumn • The Priestesses Gather Magick Brooms

Sacred Land, Sacred Sky 90

Sacred Land in America: The Great Disconnect • The Personal Politics of Place: White Euro-American Priestess, Black African Goddess, Native American Newe Land • Water from Above and Below: The Rain and the Spring • The Temple Spring and Lessons for the Priestess • Invocations and Ritual to Water • The Wind • Dancing with the Elements: Air and Ritual • Stars • Longing

Predators and Prey 111

The Goldfinch and the Bullfrog • Red-tail Feathers • Journey to the Tree • Still Life with Rabbits

CONTENTS

Peace and Activism 122

Ash Wednesday at the Nevada Test Site • There Are No Words

Living the Mysteries of Sekhmet 131

Myths • Entering Her Myth • Connecting to Her • Understanding the Sun • Days and Nights of Silence and Fast • Sekhmet in Her Temple in Nevada: The Twenty-First-Century Myth

The Final Ritual: The Heart of the Sun 149

Ritual in Honor of Sekhmet: Visioning and Re-Visioning a Ceremony • Creating Ceremony in the Twenty-First-Century • Making a Schedule • Beginning the Ceremony: Solar Fire • The Procession and Pavilion • Night of Devotion • Sunrise

Epilogue • Acknowledgments • Reading Guide

INTRODUCTION

I first learned of the Temple of Goddess Spirituality Dedicated to Sekhmet in the summer of 2004, when I discovered, on a women's spirituality listserv, a job announcement for the position of priestess. The job description stated the salary, that housing was provided, and that the responsibilities included leading rituals, being good neighbors to the Western Shoshone tribe, and having common sense.

That summer I was staying in Austin, Texas, at my sister's house, busily writing my dissertation for a PhD in Philosophy and Religion with an emphasis on Women's Spirituality at California Institute of Integral Studies. Sitting at my computer, reading and rereading the announcement, I contemplated the possibilities. Although I had been leading rituals for several years, it was only in the company of my dearest friends and in the privacy of my backyard or living room. I had performed a commitment ceremony once for two women in Seattle. I had extensive administrative experience and certainly had plenty of common sense.

The idea of living in Nevada was exhilarating. Recently my fiancé, Ben, and I had visited Las Vegas for my sister's wedding and had enjoyed ourselves immensely. Las Vegas is a great contrast to rural Oregon—the heat, bright lights, swimming pools, cleavage, and rampant hedonism.

But the part that spoke to my heart was the idea of being in service—in service to a goddess, in service to people who truly wanted to connect to the Divine. This was why in 1998 I chose to enrol in the doctoral program at California Institute of Integral Studies. I wanted to explore the Female Divine, in both academic and fully embodied approaches. I wanted to know her, the multiple "hers," and to dwell in her mystery. Facing me was a job announcement asking for someone to live that life every day, every moment.

I forwarded the job announcement to Ben. He was staying in Oregon for the summer, so I called him up: "Check your e-mail." I told him that I wouldn't apply unless he was committed to joining me should I be offered the job. A resounding "yes" echoed over the phone. He loved the desert, having attended graduate school in Arizona. He had always wanted to live out in the middle of nowhere. What touched me most was his encouragement and desire that I follow my heart.

I sent a letter of inquiry, outlining my qualifications and attaching my résumé. In the way that fortunate events can sequentially cascade when the timing is right, the founder, Genevieve Vaughan, told me she would be in Austin soon and would interview me. Ben had plans to visit me in Texas a few weeks after that, and we could drive back to Oregon by way of Las Vegas, where I could interview with the current priestess. All flowed smoothly, and by October of 2004 Ben and I moved to the temple.

What follows is a chronicle of the three years I served as priestess of the temple. As each year unfolded, my understandings of the mysteries of Sekhmet broadened and bloomed. As the ritual year coiled through its annual passage, my insight into the rhythm of the seasons deepened. I drank deeply of each moment of beauty and felt deeply each prick from the barbed thorns. As

I walked the not so well-worn path of the twenty-first-century priestess, my conception of her role gradually came into form.

A Temple in the Desert

Walking the dusty path toward the temple in the soft light of dawn, I drew my cape close against the residual chilly night air. Tonight the temple would be filled with people to celebrate the Full Moon, but now I wanted to take a moment by myself to begin my preparations to lead the ritual. As I stepped over the threshold, I realized how I yearned for the solitude of the temple in the quiet of the morning. Choosing my favorite weathered red pillow from the stack, I placed it before the deep black statue of Sekhmet and sat, feeling the cool stones of the temple floor beneath my palms.

Bright rays broke over the horizon and engulfed the soft light of dawn with the unrelenting radiance of sunrise. Golden beams illuminated the eastern door of the temple, the warm light reaching first the edge of the pillow and then my knee as the sun glided purposefully upward through the cerulean sky. I lit candles in front of the statue and ignited the charcoal underneath the kernels of frankincense. Tiny flames flickered, tendrils of scented smoke snaked through the air.

Facing the sun, I closed my eyes and opened my heart. As light filled the temple and my own body, I turned my face toward Sekhmet to chant and pray, gazing deeply into the inscrutable eyes of the black lioness.

Sekhmet in Her Desert Temple

Driving down Highway 95 north of Las Vegas on my first visit
to the temple, I missed it completely. The structure blends in
with its surroundings, seemingly a permanent part of the desert.
The temple is a small, one-story octagonal straw-bale structure,
covered in stucco and painted the sandy hue of the landscape.
Four of the walls face the cardinal directions, and inside, statues
of different goddesses sit in front of each wall. Arched doorways
on the other four walls bring the outside in from every direction.
Inside the temple in the center of the flagstone floor is a large fire
pit.

The statue of Sekhmet sits in front of the south wall, facing
north. The temple's desert surroundings make a perfect home
for the Egyptian Goddess Sekhmet. Nevada's searing heat and
blasting desert wind evoke her home in Egypt. In Egyptian iconography, Sekhmet has the head of a lioness and the body of a
woman, and her name means "female powerful one."

She sits, head crowned by the sun and the *ureaus*, a striking
cobra. She is black, gleaming in the sun that streams through
the arched doorways. The statue was made by Marsha Gomez, a
Mexican-Indian artist from Texas. With the head of a lion and a
woman's body, Sekhmet embodies all that is animal, human, and
divine. Marsha captured her very human and female nature in
her bare breasts, one slightly larger than the other. In front of her
a plaque exhorts all who enter: "May Woman be Strong as the
Lioness and Give Birth to the Future."

Across from Sekhmet in front of the north wall sits Madre
del Mundo, also made by Marsha Gomez. This statue was commissioned for the Mother's Day Peace Action at the Nevada
Test Site in 1989. She is seated with her legs crossed, holding
the Earth tenderly in her lap. On the west wall is La Virgen de

Guadalupe; she arrived with the women from Texas who came
to help build the temple. The east wall holds small statues of
goddesses on various ledges, all facing Sekhmet, representing
images of the Female Divine throughout world cultures.

The roof is open to the sky and topped by interlaced, crys-
tal-filled copper tubes that form a dome in the shape of a closed,
seven-petal lotus. When I lie on the floor of the temple and gaze
through the roof, the lotus design is like a *yantra*, a geometric
design that aids in meditation.

Genevieve Vaughan, who built the temple, created the
theory of the Gift Economy, a philosophy that takes mothering
as its example for a model of interchange, moving beyond the
pattern of exchange, when one item is traded or bartered for
another, to the paradigm of gift. Funding for the temple, retreat
center, and priestess' salary continue under Genevieve's spon-
sorship with her philosophies of feminism, peace activism, and
Goddess Spirituality as guiding principles.

Genevieve's story is iconic. On a tour of Egypt with her
husband in 1965, she visited a Sekhmet temple in Karnak. Her
guide advised her that if she wanted something she should ask
Sekhmet, and that in return she should offer a promise to the
goddess. She knew nothing of Sekhmet or Goddess Spirituality, but as she had been unable to conceive, Genevieve asked
Sekhmet for a child. In return, she promised Sekhmet that
someday she would build her a temple. Genevieve conceived
her first child only days later and over the course of years had
three daughters. A plaque in front of Sekhmet reads "A Promise
Kept."[1]

The site is truly the perfect place for a modern goddess
temple. It is in the desert but atop an aquifer; secluded, but with
easy highway access; near a large urban center, but located in the
midst of a largely uninhabited environment.

I had never lived in the desert before moving to the temple. Having settled in the Pacific Northwest for the previous decade, I imagined the desert to be stark and lifeless, even motionless. How surprising to discover that the desert around the temple teems with wildlife. Jack rabbits, owls, kangaroo rats, lizards, spiders, snakes, coyotes, and bobcats wander; hawks, ravens, buzzards, bluebirds, and goldfinches flutter and soar. Groves of fragrant creosote, mesquite trees, and salt cedars are nourished by a generous aquifer. To the east of the temple is a true oasis, the shaded Cactus Spring, a local animal watering hole and home to frogs and turtles. The spring is the source of sacred water for temple rituals.

And the nights! I have never experienced such beautiful nights. In the dark velvet of the sky, the Milky Way sweeps across and shooting stars draw wishes from my lips. The celestial heavens whisper. Mountains enfold the temple in a valley, with the Sheep Range to the east, over which the sun and moon rise, and the Spring Mountain range to the south.

My First Day and Night at the Temple

In August of 2004, Ben and I drove from Texas to Oregon and stopped at the temple for my interview with the temple priestess, Patricia Pearlman. Patricia was leaving her position at the temple due to ill health. When I met her, she walked with a cane and easily lost her breath. But her eyes were sharp as a raven's and her tongue sharper than a razor. She embodied the Crone Priestess.[2] I put on my brave interview face.

We met for lunch at the casino in Indian Springs, a few miles from the temple. Then we drove to the temple. My first feeling upon entering it was relief at seeing the statue of La Virgen de Guadalupe. I have long been devoted to her and have

traveled to the Basilica de Guadalupe many times, the cathedral built in her honor in Mexico City. Seeing La Virgen in the
temple, I knew I was in the right place. As Patricia stood in front
of Sekhmet, the bond between them became clear, her devotion
unmistakable.

Because she was having trouble walking, Patricia drove
me the short distance between the temple and the house I would
soon call home. Two old but well-kept trailers were maintained,
one for the priestess and the other a women's guest house.
These were placed around a central courtyard, surrounded by
picturesque views of the mountain ranges and the temple. It was
beautiful.

While we were together, I listened to the *herstory* of the
temple and the scope of responsibilities of the priestess. The
description of duties ranged from leading rituals to emptying
the trash cans by the spring. After talking to Patricia, I felt that
I could do the job. I had plenty of administrative and leadership
experience, I had a number of people and books to help me fill in
the missing gaps on ritual protocol, and I didn't mind emptying
trash cans. By the end of the interview I was comfortable, both
with the job and the surroundings. After Patricia left, Ben and
I pitched a tent in the courtyard to spend our first night at the
temple. And then, suddenly, this new "job" became very real.

Tucked away in our sleeping bags in our usual state of
nakedness, we listened to the night sounds and wondered about
the insects and animals living in this foreign clime. I slept
deeply, soundly, with hope for the future.

A loud blast of light and music jarred me awake. I heard the
grinding of a diesel truck engine and squinted at the bright head-
lights shining through the side of the tent. I sat up abruptly, fear
propelling me into warrior mode. Someone had driven into the
courtyard. Someone in a big diesel truck blaring music through

powerful speakers. Someone who had chosen Jimmy Buffett's "Margaritaville" to blast through the desert night.

The incongruities of this situation were lost to me as my mind filled with passionate protection of the space and overwhelming fear for my own safety. Ben, groggy with sleep, barely turned over at the disturbance. With adrenaline pumping, I pulled on my clothes and searched for the zipper to the tent door. At that moment the truck backed up and drove away, gravel crunching and music receding into the night. Ben returned to his heavy sleep, undisturbed by events. I lay there still dressed, heart thumping. My mind concocted scenario after scenario, many based on promotional trailers for horror movies.

I could barely hear myself breathe over my deafening heartbeat. Suddenly Sekhmet literally appeared in my head. My skull felt small, barely able to contain even the image of her lioness head. Her growl was low and loud like an earthquake. My heart and breath stopped. Her growl metamorphosed into words: "You will never come to harm on my land." Immediately, her image disappeared. My breath returned and my heart resumed its beat.

At the time, I did not feel a wave of comfort. I did not feel protected and cared for. I felt scared. Scared of the people who might come to the temple and wish me ill. And scared of her.

The Temple at the Crux

Later I was to discover that the placement of the temple held its deepest ironies and its most profound meanings. The temple is situated at the intersection of the sacred and profane, the spiritual and the earthly, the environment and human construction. The temple lies on liminal space, space that demarcates an edge, a threshold. In many old cultures, liminal spaces needed to be protected, and often a deity was revered at these places for protection, as was Hecate's veneration at the crossroads in Ancient Greece. Such is the threshold of the temple, where our modern demons are represented in each direction and converge with the modern sacred.

Several miles to the south of the temple lies Las Vegas. I fell under Las Vegas's spell at my first visit: the bright lights, the lavish Bellagio lobby with the kaleidoscope sky of Dale Chihuly's glass flowers floating overhead, the bountiful buffet at the Paris, the beautiful people with stunning clothes shopping at the Venetian, the dreamy and startling aerobatics of the Cirque de Soleil shows. This city held the raw hedonism missing from life in rural Oregon. The underpinnings of the luxury and excesses of the strip were visible only blocks away. One early morning I saw a drugged girl tumble out of the passenger's side of a car at the Von's grocery store on the corner of Maryland and Tropicana. The car drove away and she stumbled on.

In stark contrast to the lights of Las Vegas, north of the temple stretches over four thousand square miles of desert and mountains cordoned off as a bombing range. This range is used constantly by the American government to test the accuracy of bombs, resulting in ground-shaking, window-rattling booms. Unmanned Air Vehicles, with names like "Predator" and "Reaper," practice maneuvers daily, checking the accuracy of their bomb strikes.

East of the temple lies another front of the interminable war of human versus human, a large prison complex with two state prisons and various "boot camps" holding over three thousand "guests of the state."

West of the temple is the Nevada Test Site, truly a monument to humankind's disregard and destruction of humanity and the Earth. It is here, of course, that mushroom clouds from atomic testing were celebrated and the effects of radiation repeatedly ignored. Yucca Mountain, proposed site to dump nuclear waste, lies just a bit farther north.

Immediately across from the temple on the north side of Highway 95 is Creech Air Force Base. F-15s, F-16s, and A-10s regularly fly over, disrupting the silence with bone-jarring roars. The planes actually use the temple to line up their approach to the runway.

The land near the temple is strikingly similar to that of Afghanistan and northern Iraq, so this area is used as a training ground before troops deploy. After dark the air is lit by flares, sometimes tracing the path of bullets, other times lighting the battlefield so those engaged in war games can see one another. Black Hawk helicopters fly low over the terrain, often in groups, seemingly searching for something or someone. The Thunderbirds, the official Air Force demonstration team, practice their flashy maneuvers in the skies. A temple dedicated to peace sits in a place where one can never forget war.

Another irony of place is the temple's location on land sacred to the indigenous peoples. Millennia before the arrival of European colonists, the area comprising Yucca Mountain, Creech Air Force Base, the bombing range, and the temple was considered sacred to the Newe (or Western Shoshone) and Paiute.[3] Ancestors of the Newe are buried on Yucca Mountain, and the water in the surrounding area, including the water from Cactus Spring near the temple, is considered sacred. The Newe refer to Yucca Mountain as Snake Mountain, a place to communicate with the Great Spirit, a place where one's prayers are heard and messages are received. As told by the late Corbin Harney, Newe spiritual leader, the legend of Snake Mountain is that one day the mountain will awaken and break open and poisons will spew through the gash. Many see that as a prophecy for Yucca Mountain.

After she purchased the land, realizing she would not need all twenty acres for the temple, Genevieve Vaughn ceded the land around the temple back to the Newe people: "I gave the land back to the Shoshone, to whom it originally belonged, in a ceremony for the commemoration of the five hundred years of oppression and colonization of the Americas in 1992."[4] The temple was built in 1993 with permission from the Newe, and the land has served at times as a home base for their activities, especially when there is a peace demonstration at the Nevada Test Site.

Rituals at this temple can take on both a spiritual and political aspect. Since the 1980s, various groups have organized peace pilgrimages from Las Vegas to the nuclear test site. The groups are both secular and religious in nature, including Japanese survivors of the atomic bombings in Hiroshima and Nagasaki. The temple is a midway point for these pilgrimages. As well, Pagans from around the world make pilgrimages to the temple.

Through years of ritual, the land that holds the temple exudes a palpable sacred draw. Its numinous characteristics are fed by those who visit it and by the yearning of the land itself. People visit the temple daily. Many leave gifts for the deities, including flowers, incense, drums, sage wands, stones, shells, sacred art, statues, oils, catnip, and candles. They leave personal and sacred items, including photos, military dog tags, rings, canes, prayers written on paper, bracelets, coins, and cat toys.

Ceremonies held at the temple and the offerings strengthen the spiritual quality of the land. Once considered by many to be just another stretch of desert on the outskirts of Las Vegas, this land is now viewed as sacred. It looks sacred. It feels sacred. Has this land been made sacred through ritual and beliefs, or has its intrinsic sacredness merely been recognized through consistent ceremony? In the midst of land that is used in what many would consider to be unsacred ways, the temple is a testament to the ability of the Earth and people to connect in revered rites and to create a distinctively sacred space.

The location of the temple and its dedication to the Goddess Sekhmet bring to the fore the issue of aggression and response to aggression. Her myth outlines the struggle between aggression and protection, between balance and imbalance, in the divine order.

I have known from the beginning that the convergence of dreams, promises, and gifts in the desert speaks a message. But, in all honesty, I wasn't sure what the message was. It took a long time for these disparate pieces to come together in a whole vision, a complete understanding that I could grasp.

Sekhmet

When I began as priestess of the temple during a beautiful crisp autumn of warm days and cool nights, I knew only the basics about Sekhmet. These were easy to find; they were oft-repeated pieces that had the ring of sound bites, quips that were overly simplistic, not the multifaceted intricacies of an ancient goddess.

I had spent years researching the Mesoamerican goddesses called the Cihuateteo, the subject of my dissertation. These goddesses had been reduced to the simplistic sensationalism of "vampires" by some and "angry ghosts who steal babies" by others. Research brought to light a very different picture of these deities, one that told the story of beloved sisters who died in childbirth and were deified, honored for their bravery.

But I had not spent years researching Sekhmet. I had never been to Egypt. I had never even had a personal devotion to her. I knew the brief sound bites I found didn't tell the whole story.

And I did not know what the whole story was, either academically or personally. The lack of knowing was palpable for me.

From cursory research, I found that the icon of a lioness's head on a woman's body is ancient, as a thirty-thousand-year-old statue found in Germany testifies. Sekhmet's statues appear in many places in Egypt's history as early as 2400 BCE (5th dynasty) and continue to be found through the Greco-Roman period. During the 1300s BCE, Amenhotep III commissioned the carving of hundreds of Sekhmet statues. It is speculated that originally there were 730 statues, one for each sunrise and sunset of the year.

The figure of Sekhmet combines symbols that unite the entire cosmos. She is most definitely woman, her breasts bare, her long fingers grasping the Ankh, the Egyptian symbol of life. She is definitely animal, with a distinctive squared jaw, round ears, and whiskers. She is definitely lioness, with the short ruff of the female lion. Atop her head is the uraeus, the cobra poised to strike. Behind the uraeus the sun shines in the form of a large solar disk. The Goddess Sekhmet unites the strengths of human, animal, earth, reptile, and the cosmos.

Her name translates as "powerful" or "the female powerful one." Modern interpretations of her aspects include envisioning her as a destroyer and healer with the strength both to invoke and ward off plagues and pestilence. The statue of Sekhmet in her temple in Cactus Springs sits in front of the south wall, the sun at her back. The statue faces north, her unwavering gaze fixed on the Nevada Test Site as she sits as the Protector of the Divine Order.

Most frequently, Sekhmet is associated with the myth entitled "The Destruction of Humanity." In this myth, a group of humans rebel against Re (sometimes spelled "Ra"), the Egyptian solar deity. Re then sends his Eye to suppress the rebellion. The "Eye of Re," or the Eye of the Sun, is an independent force, a unique personage who represents the manifestation of Re's, or the sun's, power. The Eye of the Sun, in the form of the Goddess Hathor, slays the band of rebels, and with this act Hathor becomes Sekhmet. Re worries that Sekhmet will destroy the rest of humanity, so he forms a plan to intoxicate her, thereby saving humanity. Re commands seven thousand jars of barley beer, brewed by women, to be mixed with red ochre, turning it the color of blood. They pour the red brew into the field. When Sekhmet arrives, she finds the grounds brimming with "blood" and drinks until she is too intoxicated to even recognize humans. Thus, the destruction of humanity is averted.[5]

Worldwide, there are any number of myths that portray deities destroying their creations. The myth of Noah and the Flood is one example. In these myths, the deity that is powerful enough to create is powerful enough to destroy, and in the "Destruction of Humanity" myth, that power is the purview of female deities. Here, Hathor/Sekhmet is called by Re to quell rebellion, but her power is beyond the control of the male gods. She is subdued by an intoxicant because she cannot be subdued by force. In this instance, her power can be likened to the force of nature, wild and indiscriminate.

It is from this myth that Sekhmet is seen as the embodiment of anger and retribution and as an indiscriminate killer overcome by bloodlust. As well, this myth is like so many that show women governed solely by their emotions, dangerously wild and out of control.

As a feminist scholar of goddesses, I knew that this myth was more complicated than a goddess's bloodlust satiated by alcohol. Myths are commonly used for political ends, and certainly parts of the myth "The Destruction of Humanity" had social and political implications, most likely serving the goals of whoever commissioned the carving. My cursory research had not overturned an academic feminist reading of this myth. But in my new role as priestess, what had been placed before me were a temple and a goddess, and the opportunity to know her personally and intimately.

First Month

The mere thought of devoting myself to a goddess who filled my head and whose growl rumbled my bones as deeply as an earthquake was intimidating. But there was plenty to do to keep my mind off that growl. Back in Oregon, Ben and I packed a U-Haul. Ben mowed the lawn, handed our good friend and now house sitter the keys a couple of bags of cat food, and we left. I had not even had time—truthfully, I did not take the time—to think how anxious I was about the prospect of being the Priestess of Sekhmet.

We arrived in Las Vegas a day later and picked up the keys from Patricia. After a quick trip to the grocery store, we drove to our new home, where someone had already left gifts and cards on the front porch. We felt warmly welcomed.

During our second evening at the temple, a local Pagan group, Vegas Vortex, arrived for their annual all-night fire ceremony, "Bone Dance." It was at this event that I saw the spectacular and heart-felt merging of Pagan thought and Las Vegas talent and costuming with a slight edge of Burning Man.[6] A parade of feather boas, spangled spandex, sparkling lip gloss, jingling belts, rich velvets, and flowing capes crowded the temple grounds. At the opening ceremonies, Ben and I were introduced to the crowd of over a hundred. We were welcomed by hearty applause followed by a number of people relating their personal stories of being at the temple. I glimpsed the scope of my new position and the importance of the temple to this community.

Following that, the ceremonial fire was lit in a pit outside the temple and everyone circled the fire until sunrise: dancing, running, walking, skipping, singing, and chanting throughout the night. Not long after midnight fatigue overtook Ben and me, and we retreated to our bed in our new home to sleep to the sound of drums and then awaken to the sound of drums. There was something so comforting about hearing the drums in the distance and so heartening about a large group of people gathering for spiritual expression. It was a different world from rural Oregon, where a couple of close friends would join me in the backyard to celebrate the turning of the seasons.

A few weeks later, the next ritual at the temple was Samhain, or Hallowe'en. Often considered to be the "Witches' New Year," Samhain is arguably the most popular Pagan[7] holiday, possibly because it is the only Pagan holiday that coincides with the American pop culture holiday. This is the one time of year where the stores are full of Pagan-ish stuff, and everyone is talking about the dead and witches. Other Christian festival days, Christmas and Easter, coincide with events in the yearly Pagan ritual cycle, commonly referred to as The Wheel of the Year, but the pop-culture emphasis is on the Christian festival, not the Pagan one. On Samhain, the Pagan and popular cultures meet, and it's the one time of the year that it is actually fun to be a witch.

On the other hand, for Pagans it is hard to see a major religious holiday turned into a caricature where ancestors are presented as zombies and witches frighten children. The way that Hallowe'en has been commercialized is similar to the way Christmas has been hijacked by rampant consumerism; ,its meaning lost in the flurry of shopping.

Attending ritual on Samhain night is akin to Christians
going to church on Easter. All the solitary practitioners come
out and gather with the group practitioners. The meet-and-greet
before the ritual is a hubbub of conversation and catching up on
news and juicy tidbits of gossip. And, like Easter, Samhain is the
day everyone wears their best clothes. For Christians, Easter is
all about hats, heels, gloves, ties, and pastel dresses. For witches,
Samhain is all about dramatic capes of sinuous fabrics like satin
and velvet, flowing dresses that sweep the ground, and even
pointy hats. Everyone is laden with jewelry, maybe showing off
a new pentacle pendant with an amethyst in the center encircled
with a Celtic knot.

Samhain would be my introduction to those who regularly
came to the temple. Patricia had been priestess for ten years, and
I would be the third. The first priestess, Cynthia Burkhardt, had
been here for the first year, but it was Patricia who created the
legacy. I had big shoes to fill.

Thinking of the evening to come, I felt that my years in college administration had prepared me for navigating the social
aspects of the evening. But I really could not show up to Samhain in a navy suit and pumps. As I stared blankly at my closet,
my confidence level plummeted. Just one year before I came to
the temple, most of my belongings had been destroyed in a fire,
including the few ritual clothes I owned, all of my scarves, and
most of my jewelry. People would expect that I wear exquisite
ritual garb and jewelry fitting of a priestess. But we had just
moved, money was tight, and I didn't know anyone well enough
to borrow an outfit. I always take care with my dress; it is where
I draw confidence. But tonight, it just wasn't going to be anything special, and I could only hope my winning smile would
overshadow my lackluster attire. To make matters worse, it was
cold outside at night and all I had to keep myself warm were my

parka-like Oregon jackets. I didn't have a cape or even a pentacle necklace. I settled on a black skirt and black sweater with a nondescript coat.

Patricia conducted the ritual. The temple was packed inside, with people gathered around the doors peering in. The night was cold and many people wore heavy capes, the lustrous velvets reflecting the firelight. Jewelry twinkled. The fire crackled and the scent from the burning cedar logs filled the air. I followed as Patricia led the ritual, aware of all the eyes on me. I tried to be in the moment but my thoughts wandered to the future. How would it be when I led these rituals? Patricia was sure and confident as the seasoned crone. I didn't know.

Patricia brought out a plate with a halved pomegranate. We each took a seed and pondered the mystery—the mystery of Persephone's entry to the underworld, the mystery of our own entry into winter, the dark half of the year. My thoughts swirled.

At the end of the ceremony, she officially handed over the "reins" in the guise of a tambourine with streamers, a fitting symbol as we each followed the beat of our own drum. Ben and I were encircled by warm welcomes from well-wishers clad in swirling capes and jingling bracelets.

Pagans usually end ceremonies with the phrase: "Merry meet, merry part, and merry meet again." We felt well met. There was a sense of camaraderie, excitement, and newness. My thoughts still swirled, but somewhere an inner sense of confidence began to swell. I felt a sense of rightness—I was in the right place at the right time. My round peg fit this round hole.

Though I did not know it at the time, this would be the last ritual Patricia would lead at the temple. Over the next year, her health worsened dramatically. She crossed over in the spring of 2006. She is still missed.

"I Am Black"

My first few weeks at the temple were occupied by basic chores: cleaning and organizing. The houses had been unoccupied for a few months between Patricia's departure and my arrival, and a number of desert creatures had decided to take up residence. Mice were everywhere, leaving the marks of their tiny teeth on every wood and plastic item in the kitchen. Large, hairy yet harmless wolf spiders roamed the ceiling, challenging me to conquer my own baseless, irrational fears. There were other mundane tasks at hand, one of the most complicated being arranging fast and reliable Internet access without benefit of cable or improved phone lines.

Within a few weeks of my arrival at the temple, Genevieve sponsored a conference on the Gift Economy to be held in Las Vegas. During the conference, two women stayed at the guest house. One was Kalli Rose Halvorson, my friend and astrologer for many years. Kalli Rose was a native Oregonian, and her physique mirrored her Scandinavian roots: tall, with powerful hands and eyes that reflected both compassion and fierce steely strength.[8]

The night before the opening session, the three of us went to sit in the temple and make a fire. It was a clear, cool, starfilled night, and I reveled in the company of women who shared similar worldviews. Though I can't remember the third woman clearly, I do remember her voice. Her words floated above the crackling fire, asking me what I myself most wanted to know, a request for which I had no true response. She said, "Tell us about Sekhmet."

I didn't know how to answer. I loathed repeating a myth that I didn't have the academic background to contextualize. I was all too aware that the knowledge of the mind is of limited use in understanding the Mystery, the Infinite, the Paradox, and the Great Unknown, but I was also painfully aware that I didn't know Sekhmet with my body or my heart.

Feelings of inadequacy rolled over me in a suffocating wave. My only answer was: "I've just started here. I'm not sure."

How banal. I felt stupid, and worse, I felt like a charlatan, an imposter. What the hell was I thinking? That I could be a priestess to a goddess I didn't even know?

The fact that I'd put so much time and effort into housekeeping, working to clean and organize everything, seemed the actions of a neophyte, not a priestess. As for the people who had noticed the changes I made on the web page—well, let's just say the feedback was not overwhelmingly positive. I tried to stop that train of thought. That was not true. I had received both positive and negative feedback on the web page. People had noticed the work I had done around the temple and on the grounds and were very appreciative.

Now that train of thought was idling, though still there on the tracks. Here I was, in the temple with two kindred sisters, and I had no idea what to say or do about the goddess who sat right in front of me, the goddess of this temple. The words *charlatan* and *imposter* whispered over and over in my head.

And then, the greatest blessing happened. The woman whose name I can't remember suggested that we try something she had done in temples before. We sat in circle around the fire, grounded and centered ourselves, and then we opened our hearts, our ears, and our minds to Sekhmet. We asked her to communicate with us.

I have no memory of what Sekhmet spoke to me that night. My only memory is of my immense relief that somebody had figured out something to do. When we had completed our meditation, we each described what we had heard. Kalli Rose said, "Sekhmet came to me, and she said, 'I am Black.' "

This message has stayed with me over the years. I return to it again and again. What did she mean? She is black, as in her race, the color of her skin? Perhaps she is African, an African goddess. Her statue in the temple is black, as are the original Egyptian statues of Sekhmet, carved from diorite. Diorite is a black igneous stone whose fire-wrought origins affirm her connection to earth and fire, world and sun. High iron content in Egyptian diorite not only gives the stone a black color but also adds richness to the sediment that contributes to the Nile's renowned fertility. For ancient Egyptians, the color black connoted two complementary aspects of the underworld—fertility and death. The link of the color black with fertility was underscored with the rich fertile black soil the Nile delivered with its annual inundation. Black symbolized Egypt itself, as the word for black, *kem*, is the root for the name of the Egyptian people, *kememu* (black people), and the land, *Kemet* (black land).

"I am Black."

My thoughts followed her lead as I looked within:

She is black, the night. She is black, the impenetrable Mystery. She is black, the origin of all life. She is black, the rich fecund earth. She is black, the darkness of the womb. She is black, the deepest sky. She is black; she is powerful. She is the convergence of all things. She envelops me. She is black.

My First Public Ritual

The Gift Economy Conference attracted luminaries from around the globe. Many of the speakers were women whose books I had read, whose careers I had followed, and who had passionately inspired me, both academically and emotionally. And Genevieve had invited them to the temple for a ritual. Assuming she would lead the ritual, I met with Patricia at her apartment in Las Vegas to discuss what small part I might play that evening. However, Patricia was insistent that I lead the ritual. Not feeling her best, she nevertheless promised to sit in the temple to watch and give moral support as I led my first public ritual.

I'm not sure how the situation could have been more intimidating. I was still reeling from the fact that I had been completely void of ideas only the night before when there were only two other women. Now, faced with the task of leading a group of women who were well versed in Goddess Spirituality—mothers of the movement, leaders in their fields—I was inundated by feelings of inadequacy, lack of preparedness, and shame for not being able to live up to my role as priestess.

I prepared a very simple ritual, based on a generic honoring of the Goddess and of Sekhmet, the latter whom I still did not know how to approach. I chose the well-known anthem of the Goddess Spirituality movement, "We All Come from the Goddess,"[9] to begin and decided to end with an affirmation of sisterhood. As I contemplated my plan, it just seemed so terribly lame, so insipidly simple—it seemed to taunt me with "first timer."

Scrutinizing my paltry choices of ritual clothing, I knew I wouldn't even look as though I knew what I was doing. I pulled on a black skirt and red shirt, her colors. I would work the "simple but devout" angle with the costuming.

I prepared the temple and the fire, trying my best to calm and center myself. Patricia sat in a corner, being her raven self, eyes alert and seemingly waiting for me to make a mistake.

Most likely that is not at all what was going on, but keeping my
emotional projections under control was a task. I lit some sage
and inhaled deeply, pleading with this friendly plant to help me.
I needed clarity, grace, charm, and above all, to be calm and
grounded.

Later than expected, the first wave of guests pulled in to the
parking lot after dark. We all milled about in the chilly night air,
waiting for the remainder to arrive. After a half hour or longer
had passed, Genevieve urged me to start the ritual anyway,
suggesting I could lead two rituals that evening. So I called the
group inside the temple.

In the firelight, I could make out faces in the circle. My
eyes swept around the temple and stopped on a familiar face.
My mind balked at comprehending her identity, but in moments
I knew. It was Luisah Teish, world-renowned ritualist. This
woman, a Yoruba Chief, priestess, and one of the founding mothers of the Women's Spirituality movement, stood in the circle.
She would be witness to the very first public ritual that I would
perform. This wasn't how I had planned to make my début.

The composition of this group was quite different from
the group at Samhain. There were fewer people, only fifteen
or twenty, all women, all academics, hailing from diverse
areas around the globe: Europe, Africa, the Americas, Pacific
Islands, Asia. Overall, their ritual wear was more subdued, just a
necklace here and there. A few women wore more elaborate ceremonial attire. Teish was draped in richly colored African cloth,
looking regal and beautiful and every inch a priestess. Reaching
deep, I scraped together the dregs of my self-confidence, put on
my brave face again, opened my heart as wide as I could, and
gathered the women around the fire.

We circled together as sisters, and I initiated the singing of

"We All Come from the Goddess." Instead of being trite, it was known and comforting, a song that united these women from all over the globe. We went around the circle, each one offering a prayer.

And it was beautiful. The women in the circle opened their hearts to one another, relishing the splendor of the starry night and the shared company. Teish's smile soothed my soul and the curve of Patricia's lips was inscrutable. I heard the next wave of guests arrive, gravel crunching under the tires. I walked out to meet them in the darkness, my heart full and open.

A few days later, I exchanged e-mails with Teish. She answered my e-mail with the salutation: "Dear Sister Priestess." I knew then that I had stepped over a threshold.

Daily Life of a Twenty-First-Century Priestess

My life at the temple slid into a pattern, a pattern that in some ways was eerily similar to my former life as a college administrator. I began work not long after sunrise, turning on the computer to answer e-mail, update the website, and deal with inquiries and problems. Just as I used to do at the college, I arranged gatherings and meetings, dealt with internecine quarrels and politics, and tried to put out fires while they were small.

But the calendar and the environment were radically different. When I worked in an office, most of my daily interactions were electronic and mechanical rather than physical. I talked to people on the phone or by e-mail; I commuted in my car; I kept up on news and gossip through the Internet. My work day usually corresponded to the eight-to-five schedule with many late work nights. My schedule was determined by the academic calendar, so my year was a series of beginnings with each new term in September, January, March, and June.

My work environment and calendar as a priestess were very different. Instead of being inside an office or classroom most of the day, I was out in the elements leading rituals. My life became entwined with the land, the wind, the sun, the rain, the cold, the heat, and the stars. And the rhythm of my work life changed drastically. Instead of living by a twelve-month calendar with only a passing connection to natural cycles, I lived by the ritual schedule and rode the tides of the solar and lunar paths. My year was a series of beginnings, but of seasons instead of school terms beginning in November, February, May, and August.

I shifted from working inside in a temperature-controlled environment to working outside in the weather, and from living by a contrived calendar to living with the natural seasonal calendar. These two shifts influenced me remarkably, tying my daily life with the land.

I watch the sun approach the western horizon and feel relief at the sound of the sharp click as I turn off the computer at the end of this day of miscommunications and misunderstandings. I kiss Ben good-bye, pick up my basket, and take the dusty path from my house to the temple. Lying on the sun-warmed stone floor of the temple and looking through the lotus yantra above, I surrender to this day, this day of protecting my heart. The Earth holds me in her hand, and the petals of my heart open to the sky, to the sun and stars. The spirit of life and love enters my body, and I am rejuvenated.

Typical Day

In the morning, I awaken to the spreading light of dawn. Ben and I usually sleep outside on the Starbed, a platform six feet off the ground, giving protection from the desert crawlers like snakes and scorpions. Dawn is the coolest time of the day, so in the summers we luxuriate in the fresh cool air. Until I started sleeping outside I never really thought about the space of time between twilight and sunrise. The sky becomes lighter incrementally, slowly, and sumptuously. In the summer, dawn creeps in

increasingly early, before 5:00 a.m. on the days around the summer solstice. Hues of red and gold deepen in the sky and then
everything slowly washes to light. At that point, the brilliant gold
of the sun breaks over the horizon—a crescent at first, then fully
illuminated like an impossibly burnished gold disc. We squint at
the glimmering light, the warmth coming fast. We pull the covers
over our heads for just a few more minutes of sleep. Then the
cool of the dawn dissipates as quickly as rabbits scatter, and the
heat of the sun pours down on us. Our day begins.

After breakfast, brushing my teeth, and a quick check of
e-mail, I trundle down the dusty path to the temple, carrying my
basket full of candles, incense, lighters, prayers, rags, vinegar-
and-water cleaning solution, and a small trash bag. Along the
way I sing to dried brush and twigs, wondering if any would like
to be a part of the morning fire. There are always volunteers, and
I appreciate each one.

I enter the temple and slip off my shoes, feeling the still-
cool stones. I unload my armful of brush into the fire pit and
search through my basket for incense and charcoal. I light the
charcoal and blow it to a bright burning crimson, then place a bit
of frankincense resin on a piece of foil. Once the foil is placed
on the glowing charcoal, wispy smoke curls upward, spreading
fragrance like perfumed strands of silk floating in the air. I turn
to light the brush in the fire pit for a short quick burst of flame in
honor of Sekhmet, the solar goddess.

I pull up a weathered red pillow and seat myself in front
of Sekhmet, my back to the fire. I look up into her eyes, and
breathe myself into this space, into her temple, as her priestess.
My consciousness first sinks into the stones of the temple floor,
pooling underneath me and grounding in this space, connecting
to the aquifer below. Then I move into myself, my body, here
and now. I feel the fire warm on my back. My consciousness

moves through me, up my spine and through my head. I look up through the open-weave roof of the temple to the sapphire sky above. I close my eyes and am connected above and below.

I look toward Sekhmet, my eyes and heart open. I breathe this consciousness. I chant Sekhmet's mantra, *Sa Sekhem Sahu,* opening myself to the life-bringing breath of the strength and the power of the fire without and within, to become a fully realized being. I say her names and end with the names of those who have asked for prayers. Then I get up and take a look around and assess what needs to be cleaned and picked up today.

Because the roof and doors of the temple are open, birds, mice, and other desert critters wander through, so there is always something to be cleaned. Some parts of the daily routine are straightforward: sweeping the stones, cleaning bird droppings off the floor, scraping wax from rocks and shelves, cleaning and refilling candle holders, burning offerings of flowers that are past their prime, washing flower vases, dusting off statues, refilling pamphlets, restocking incense, and generally tidying up. And always I find new offerings.

Animal, Vegetable, Mineral Offerings

Though I would usually go to the temple in the morning and at sunset, most of the time the temple sits open, waiting, and unattended. This is, I believe, a part of the magick and beauty of this temple—that it is open to anyone. It makes the temple a unique and extraordinary place. It also answers a very interesting but most likely unasked question: In a culture such as modern, Protestant-leaning America, where giving offerings is an unusual act and places of religious worship are not usually open to the public, what do people do in a temple where there is no posted protocol for offerings and no one around to direct their actions?

People come, most often singly, and leave offerings. Every day I find some assortment of candles, plastic flowers, fresh flowers, jewelry, sage wands, beer, art, and photos carefully placed in the temple. Most often these items are left in front of a particular goddess, the intention clear. One day I found a tiny silver pendant in the shape of a knife, the miniature handle curved and the blade straight, resting in the lap of Sekhmet—an offering honoring one of Sekhmet's many names, "Sekhmet of the Knives." I regularly found sage bundles in front of Madre del Mundo, offerings linked with her Native American roots.

What to do with all of these offerings? At first, I tried an administrative solution, meaning an across-the-board decree: all offerings would be either burned or buried at the turn of each season. But then, some offerings begged to have different outcomes. And so I moved from a blanket policy to a case-by-case process, with established precedents, of course.

Flowers were the easiest. Flowers are a traditional offering for deities, probably because they are beautiful, scented, and even when cut retain a spark of life. I left vases inside and there was usually a water bottle or two around to fill the vase. When the flowers passed their prime, I offered them in prayer in a ceremonial fire. I think fresh flowers are one of the best offerings because of their heady scent and vivacious colors. As they need to be replaced periodically, fresh flowers also show a continued devotion. And, when burned, they provided a final offering in the fire. They are probably the most traditional offering worldwide.

Plastic flowers are a different matter. Plastic flowers provide color and beauty not found in the desert landscape, and they are inexpensive, even available at the mini-mart in the gas station in Indian Springs, the closest town to the temple. Plastic flowers provide the gift of beauty and color, but they do not provide scent or any sense of life.

For my priestess duties, plastic flowers were a conundrum. They did not naturally disintegrate, nor did I think it wise to burn them, so when people left plastic flowers, I would take them out at the next turn-of-the-season clearing and bury them alongside other nonburnable offerings.

Incense and candles were also popular offerings. These offerings, like flowers, follow ancient traditions. Incense burns and releases a sweet smoke that drifts skyward, making it a perfect offering for the deities. Candles hold the spark of life, the flame. Frankincense, myrrh, and *kyphi*[10] were popular incense scents left for Sekhmet as they had been used in Egypt, and rose incense was left in honor of La Virgen de Guadalupe. Many people brought candles to the temple, often beautiful tapers and votives. However, in the summer when temperatures regularly soared above 100°F and frequently over 110°F, candles would melt quickly and often drip all over the rocks on the floor, giving me something else to clean. I preferred that people bring tea lights or novena candles because they are self-contained.

I was always so appreciative when people left incense and tea lights in the temple for others to use because not everyone came to the temple prepared, and once they are inside, the urge to light candles and incense is instinctual.

Another traditional offering is food. All sorts of foods were left as offerings at the temple: apples, strawberries, cakes, honey, nuts, meat, to name only a few. I burned all the food offerings in the temple fire pit, usually after the mice and other critters had had their feast. Though one time, an offering of a dozen or so papayas became the center of a feast for the ravens. And what a feast it was! The ravens picked at the papaya and flung bits of it all around the temple, on the statues, everywhere. I was cleaning up bits of papaya for weeks. After that, I remembered not to let fruit sit too long in the temple.

Liquid offerings abounded, especially juice and beer. These
I poured out at the feet of the goddess in front of whom they had
been left. Because of Sekhmet's association with beer, and most
specifically red beer, I would often find six-packs of Killian's
Red beer left for her. And every month or so, someone would
come and leave a case or two of bottled water. I would pour out a
bottle as an offering then bring the remainder to the guest house.

Jewelry was another frequent offering. Rings and necklaces
were left on the statues, adornments for the goddesses. After a
certain time I removed the offerings from the statues. At times
I buried them, and sometimes I took the whole piece of jewelry
and kept it in a box for a special ritual when that particular
goddess's statue would be adorned. If the jewelry was made of
beads, I often restrung a few different offerings together to create a beautiful adornment for the statue. If the offering had glass
or semiprecious stone beads, I might cut the string and mix the
beads with the stones of the temple floor.

The offerings that couldn't be burned or poured were buried. Placing things within the earth is an act of nourishing the
Earth, honoring her cycles—the continual nourishment of life-
death-life. The Earth transmutes the energy of these offerings,
bringing them into her cycles.

In the dry clay earth around the temple, it was no easy task
to dig holes large enough to bury offerings. Fortunately, Ben
was always willing to swing the pickax and dig a deep hole. One
time I dug the hole for some offerings, so it was not very deep.
I cut myself on a shard of pottery to be buried, and I bled on the
offerings. Though I worked to cover them thoroughly, they were
uncovered by some beast the following night. The second burial,
executed by Ben, went as planned. The items stayed buried.

In a way, it was ironic. While so often ceremonies are centered on the idea of infusing something with energy, my work

with offerings at the temple was focused on defusing and transmitting energy. Too many offerings, too many intentions, too many personal heart-felt prayers, too many tears began to add up in the relatively small temple space. I would cleanse the temple regularly, both physically and energetically, to keep the space open, willing, and ready to receive the new.

One bright morning I walked into the temple to find a photo in a large wooden frame with wrought-iron bars across the front. The photo seemed to be someone's promotional shot as an exotic dancer. It was accompanied by a note in which she explained that she was seeking the protection of the temple. The framed photo stayed in the temple by the west door and I burned a candle in front of it for her. After a few weeks, I buried it whole with the prayer that she would always be protected. I took her photo out of the frame so that she would not be imprisoned but rather protected by the embrace of the land.

One of the largest offerings left was a painting on canvas and a manuscript for a book detailing the tragedies of the author's life. Her pain, horror, and anguish emanated from the manuscript and the painting. After much contemplation, I decided to burn them both, seeking to release the artist from her past and to release her mind from the idea that her anguish was the best or only fuel for her art.

Sometimes the offerings left me with my own sense of despair, anguish, and responsibility. I tried to intuit the best possible course of action with each offering, wanting to honor the wishes of someone I had never met.

One particularly poignant offering was a dead lizard, wrapped neatly in a cloth and tucked in a shoebox. Inside the box along with the lizard were a T-shirt, the lizard's watering bottle, and some food. This box was placed lovingly in front of the statue of Madre del Mundo. I cried when I found it. Ben dug a deep hole and we buried the lizard near the temple.

There were times when offerings needed to be broken. Some items held great strength and energy, and I felt that it was better for that energy to be released. When I broke an offering, I did it with a prayer that the energy infused in it would be released and support the highest good. Breaking an item never meant that I disregarded it. The most difficult offering that I had to break was a candlestick in the shape of Sekhmet. It had very strong magick, very beautiful love magick woven into it. But it was the turn of the season, and this offering had already been in the temple one extra season, so it was time to move it along. I dug its own special hole, and as I placed it into the hole I prayed that its love would be released and nourish the Earth. When my spade hit the candlestick and it broke, I could feel the waves of love move out.

Not long after I began my service as priestess, I encountered one offering that was particularly memorable; it had an imma-nent power yet was also a little creepy. The offering was left on what we called the "moon rock," a large, white boulder situated on the short path approaching the south entrance of the temple. On full moon nights the moonlight illuminates the rock and it gleams brightly. There is a deep indentation on the top and, just as Patricia did, I collected the rainwater that accumulated in the indentation when it rained on full moon nights, an extraordinary occurrence considering how little rain we received.

I went out to the temple one morning and noticed some small odd squiggly bits in the moon rock's indentation. I looked closer and was struck by their familiarity. Over the years I have been the beneficiary of many gifts from cats, often left on the front porch, and these squiggly bits looked familiar, like rodent entrails. There was also a small amount of blood on the rock. I put my hand on the rock, nearby but not on the entrails—I am squeamish about those sorts of things. When my hand rested on the rock, my head instantly went fuzzy, like a TV screen after the station has signed off. I knew I had to be careful with this offering.

In retrospect, I would have handled the situation differently, say, smudging with Palo Santo and rinsing the rock with water from the spring. But at that time, only a few months after I had come to the temple, I relied on what I had learned from my grandmother about how to clean. I trotted back to the house to get my trusty magick rubber gloves and called on the lessons of my grandmother and the smell of clean I learned from her—Clorox Bleach. With gloved hands I removed and buried the entrails, then set about cleaning the rock, hoping that was the right thing to do. I had the distinct feeling that the offering was beneficial—powerful with no ill intent. As I wiped the indentation of the moon rock, I recognized the power and intention of the offering, honoring whoever had left this with palpable love and purpose.

My thoughts return to one dark and clear November night. Ben and I are wending our way home from an evening in Las Vegas, and as we come down Highway 95 and draw close to the temple we can see light streaming from the doorways and beaming through the roof. Immediately fear and anger well up in my chest—is there an uncontrolled fire inside? No one is supposed to be in the temple after dark without calling me first. As we speed up the dirt road, I see that there are no cars in the parking lot and my fear surges—has someone set fire to the temple and then left? Before the car stops, I jump out and sprint across the sand up to the temple.

I reach the doorway and stop in my tracks as I am met with a beautiful sight. The temple is steeped in light

*emanating from thirteen novena candles glowing in front
of La Virgen de Guadalupe. A circle of salt rounds the
fire pit, designating it as a sacred and protected area. I
stand in the cold night air, breathing in the space filled
with passionate intent galvanized by love. An ardent
petitioner has been here. I begin chiding myself for the
anger I had held earlier for the illicit visitor, and my
heart swells to have come home to the temple filled with
radiance and the magick of someone's ritual that now
nourishes this sacred space.*

The Folk

A s a public place with a multi-focus mission, the temple
draws an eclectic array of people who gather for ritual. The
circle usually consists of fifteen to twenty-five people for Full
Moon ceremonies, five to ten for New Moons, and thirty to fifty
for the Solar rituals. Those who come to the temple fit the pattern
of the modern American Pagan—most raised at least nominally
Christian, predominately Euro-American with some education.
The ratio of female-to-male attendance for most rituals is about
60 percent female to 40 percent male. Whenever I met with other
clergy, they were always surprised at this statistic because the
percentage of men attending the temple is actually higher than
in many Christian sect services. Those who come to ritual typically are from the surrounding areas—Las Vegas, Pahrump, and
Indian Springs—but because of its prominence as one of the few
goddess temples, our temple attracts visitors from all over the
world, including many luminaries in Goddess Spirituality.

Attendees at temple rituals cut a wide swath, including the
usual suspects: Pagans, Wiccans, and Goddess Worshippers, not
necessarily inclusive or exclusive of one another. Pagan is the
broadest category, which covers adherents of any non-Abraha-
mic religion, essentially meaning that anyone who is not Jewish,
Christian, or Muslim is considered Pagan. The members of the
lively and diverse Pagan scene in Las Vegas hold the temple

dearly in their hearts. Wicca is a subset of Paganism, often considered to be a modern form of witchcraft. Much of modern Wicca is based on traditions from the British Isles. Many, but not all, modern practitioners regard Wicca as specifically the tradition formed by Gerald Gardner and its spinoff, Alexandrian Wicca. Wicca is usually considered duo-theistic, honoring a goddess and a god.

Goddess Spirituality can be considered a subset of Paganism or Wicca, although some practitioners would argue that it is a stand-alone tradition. Sometimes referred to as Dianic Wicca, Goddess Spirituality centers on the honoring of the Female Divine in all of her aspects. Influential leaders of this movement, like Starhawk and Z Budapest, have beautifully entwined political activism with spiritual practice, giving women a spiritual path. Not all followers of Goddess Spirituality would self-identify as Wicca. Thealogically, the temple is centered in the Goddess Spirituality tradition.

The temple attracts activists of all faiths and activists of no faiths. It has strong ties with the peace and justice movements, and especially close ties with a variety of atheistic and theistic grassroots groups. The temple works closely with Nevada Desert Experience, a Las Vegas-based Catholic Worker group. It is not unusual to find a nun or priest staying at the temple, a situation many would find odd. But with respect to peace activism, our differences are minimal and our goals united. There is also a feminist contingent of those who identify with the philosophical stance of the temple but do not necessarily adhere to any spiritual practice.

The goddesses in the temple also draw a variety of people. Because of the temple's focus on Sekhmet, it attracts Kemetic Reconstructionists—those who reconstruct ancient Egyptian spiritual practice. I always felt a bit under scrutiny with these guests because my knowledge of Egyptian ritual was cursory at best.

Sometimes a stray Guadalupana who is definitely not Pagan stops by the temple to pay homage to the statue of La Virgen de Guadalupe. One year we held a ceremony on December twelfth, the traditional day she is honored in Mexico. The ceremony was in English and Spanish, with an eclectic mix of Pagans and Catholics in attendance.

I am sure the discerning reader can by now see that the people attending ritual at the temple are not a homogenous group. Congregants often follow a mix of ancient and modern traditions, with sometimes clashing beliefs. Probably the most frequent criticism comes from those following a Wiccan tradition who feel, and sometimes vociferously express, that to leave out the god is absurd, if not sacrilegious. As well, some Pagans do not support the intertwining of politics and spirituality, especially the interweaving of feminism and peace activism.

And then there are the curious folks. Because the temple's rituals are public and open, unusual for Pagan ceremonies, they provide an opportunity for people to join who might otherwise never participate in ritual.

One of the most memorable in this category was the UFO chaser. Probably in his mid-thirties, fit and handsome, he was camping on the Bureau of Land Management (BLM) land near the temple, saw some activity, and thought he'd join in. At first I thought he had spent a little too much time in the sun. He worked part of the year to save up enough money to come out to the desert to try to contact UFOs, mainly using large bright lights. He said that he wanted to contact them because he believed they could help save our planet, that our civilization was on an inevitable track to self-destruction. As I got to know him, I found him to be one of the kindest, most open-hearted people I have met,

working in his way for the greater good. I was ashamed at my
narrow and judgmental first impression.

**Visitors to the Temple: The Random and the Not Well Inten-
tioned**

The temple area is located on the edge of a large expanse of
uninhabited desert as well as along a lonely stretch of Highway
95. If someone was stranded on the highway or in the desert, our
house was the first they would approach. This happened far more
frequently than I would have imagined. One early morning when
I was at the temple, chanting, I saw a man and woman stumbling
out of the desert. She carried a pair of high-heeled white shoes,
her blue dress smudged with dust. Sand covered his dark blue
jeans and his unbuttoned shirt lay open. They did not approach
the temple, but continued walking toward the highway, giggling.

Right after lunch one warm spring day, a middle-aged man
dressed in a suit and tie knocked at our door. Dust was ground
into his lined face, his dark suit was dusted in light-colored sand,
and his dress shoes were wrecked beyond repair. In halting English, he explained that he was coming back from an interview
in Pahrump, a city to the southwest of us. The trip is about 140
miles by highway, but someone had told him that it would be
quicker to take a shortcut, which turned out to be an unimproved
off-road vehicle trail. His car had bottomed out in a ravine, and
he walked for hours through the desert. Ours was the first house
he had seen. He politely asked if he could have some water. We
took him to Indian Springs so he could call a tow truck.

In the summer of 2004, we took a short vacation and headed
back to Oregon. On our return trip, our flight was delayed and
we did not get back to our desert house until after 2:00 a.m.
Oddly, a light was on and the door was bolted from the inside.

We knocked at our door, hoping whoever was inside would let us in. A middle-aged woman with unkempt curly blond hair peered through the glass and finally opened the door. She said she had come to the temple and someone told her that she could stay here. I led her over to the guest house so she could sleep there instead of on our couch.

After she was tucked away, Ben and I looked around our house. Open tuna fish cans cluttered the kitchen counter. Dirty dishes were scattered about. We headed off to bed, knowing we would be cleaning in the morning. The next day, with clearer heads, we started noticing other things about the house. The notebook on Ben's desk was filled with nonsensical, journal-like entries of remembered places and numbers and names that did not form a coherent whole. There were sticky notes tacked on the sliding glass door, filled with more carefully written yet illogical sentences. We began to suspect that our guest was not just messy.

I went over to the guest house to talk with her. She cleared up the mystery of the tuna cans, telling me that she knew she had to feed the cats and that was the only food she could find. No wonder the cats seemed nonplussed about her presence, probably grateful for a break from dry food. These coherent thoughts were followed by ramblings about a real estate agent who had told her our house was for sale. This agent had let her into our house and told her to stay here. Once the conversation took this turn, I began to think that she needed more help than I could give her. She suddenly began gathering her things to leave, bundling up with layer after layer even though it was over 80°F outside in the early morning.

I went back to my house and called 911. I told the operator that I could drive her to a hospital in Las Vegas, but the operator told me that under no circumstances should I be alone in the car with her. I was to have her wait until an officer arrived. I went back to the guest house to detain her, but she was already leaving, marching past me to the highway on her way to Reno. When the officer arrived and heard the story, he drove toward Reno, hoping to find her before she fainted in the already searing desert morning.

Later, Ben and I read the notes she had left, and for months afterward we found more notes tucked around the house. They revealed an educated (her grammar and spelling were flawless) but disorganized and incoherent mind. I never found out more about her story, though I'm sure the cats still regard her with affection after feasting on solid white albacore.

One beautiful afternoon, the azure sky an ideal backdrop for the brilliant golden sun and scattered puffy white clouds, the wind whipping about, I sat in my living room, grading papers the old-fashioned way with pen and paper. I was teaching a Women's Studies course at the College of Southern Nevada. While I was searching for inspiration on how to tell a certain student that her essay lacked a coherent thesis, I gazed through the window at the temple. Something fluttered and caught my eye. There seemed to be a flag or piece of cloth caught on one of the turrets of the temple. For a few moments I watched it whip in the wind. As I stared, the form took shape, and I realized I was looking at a man sitting on the roof of the temple, his shirt thrashing wildly. I dropped my papers, shoved my feet into my sandals, and ran out the door and down the path to the temple.

I could clearly see a man in his twenties, sitting on the roof of the temple, gazing out to the south, oblivious to me. When I was close enough, and I heard my words carry loudly with my mother's most imperious school administrator's voice: "You are so not supposed to be up there! Come down right now!" He turned to me, eyes wide, and scampered down immediately. I put my hands on my hips in satisfaction, silently thanking my mother.

At first I was furious that this young man had scaled the walls of the temple, and I let him know that in no uncertain terms. But after chatting with him a bit, my heart softened with the plight of his present situation. He said he had been drawn to the temple and climbed to the top to "get a different perspective." We parted with a hug and he promised to find perspective in another manner.

In my time at the temple, there were very few visitors who were not well intentioned. But during one Samhain it was obvious that people were intentionally trying to disrupt the ritual. We gathered for the 7:30 p.m. ceremony. The dark of night had fully set in with the waxing moon well overhead, milky light illuminating the desert. I began the ritual with these words, to ground the group and cast the circle:

Feel your feet on the ground, feel roots grow from your feet into the ground, deeper and deeper into the Earth. Feel yourself as the tree trunk. Feel the trunk grow through your spine, through the crown of your head, branches growing, pushing out in all directions. Your branches reach deep into the heavens. Feel the stars grow from your branches, twinkling. Push and grow more and more stars from your branches, turning them brighter and brighter, until they light up the heavens. Move this starry light through your trunk to the Earth, through your roots. You are the world tree. You are the divine connection between the sky and the Earth. Hold hands: This is our community. These are our sisters and brothers. Look around, feel this circle, commit yourself to hold this sacred space tonight so that all may be held in safe, loving hands. Casting the circle is not always about geographic space; it is about casting ourselves into a woven circle together.

It was at this point that we heard howling. Not the howling of the coyotes but rather the howling of possibly inebriated people.

I stopped for a moment, locating the source of the noise as being near the spring. I had planned a soulful and meditative ritual for the evening, and howling partiers would not add anything positive to the mood. I leaned over and quietly asked Ben and Dean, a regular at our ceremonies, to check out what was happening and ask the partiers to hold down the noise until we finished. I knew both Ben and Dean would handle the situation with calm, clear heads. A few others joined them, and they walked to the spring while I continued with the ritual. Not long after, the howling subsided and Ben and Dean's group returned. We continued on with our ritual in the lovely sweet silence of the desert night.

Afterward, we learned what had happened. I had assumed that the people gathered at the spring were having a loud party. But instead, they were there to purposefully disrupt the ritual. When Ben and the others approached them, they fled into the trees near the spring. Dean noticed that one of the trucks had an Indian Springs Volunteer Fire Department plate. Living most of my life in rural areas, I have a high regard for and am deeply indebted to the volunteers who devote their time and risk their lives to keep us safe. I was dismayed that one of them would partake in this.

But by far the oddest protest against the temple occurred one sunny afternoon in early spring. I was working at my computer and Ben was at the other end of the house, working at his computer. We were listening to a mix of Afro-pop tunes, and I thought some of the singing seemed discordant. I got up, walked to the speaker, and realized that the discordant notes were not coming from the song but from outside. I opened the front door and clearly heard loud singing at the temple. I called to Ben as I walked out the door to see what was happening, assuming that it was some group that had come to the temple to do a ritual.

As I walked farther down the path, I could make out some of the words. "We have the keys to the gates of hell, and we will prevail." This was not the chant of a nice little group of Pagans having a ritual. I stepped up my pace, my long red skirt flapping against my legs, snagging on the shrubs along the path.

When I crested the hill, the scene that opened before me was bizarre. A group of five or six middle-aged women and men were circling and chanting in the ritual space in front of the temple while music blared from their car stereo. They were dressed in what looked like white bed sheets, holes torn for the arms, and belted with strips of cloth. I think one of them wore a hat. I knew even without hearing the chant that these were not Pagans because I couldn't imagine any group of Pagans showing up to a ritual wrapped in torn sheets.

The group turned and saw me. I stood next to the temple, tall and strong in my red dress, fully a Pagan priestess, and said, "What are you doing?" They ran to their car, falling over themselves to hurry and get the doors unlocked. I approached the car, and the man driving looked at me out the window and yelled, "We were just looking around," as they accelerated, dust flying out behind their spinning wheels. I just shook my head and laughed. And took down their Arizona license plate number, just in case.

I went back to my office and searched on the Internet for the words they had been repeating. They were from the Bible, 16:18–19, when Jesus speaks to Peter about the church. The English Standard Version reads:

And I tell you, you are Peter, and on this rock I will build my church, and the gates of hell shall not prevail against it. I will give you the keys of the kingdom of heaven, and whatever you bind on Earth shall be bound in heaven, and whatever you loose on Earth shall be loosed in heaven.

I never discovered exactly what their intention was, other than to give me one of the most humorous stories of my time at the temple. The concept of hell is Christian, not Pagan, so I didn't worry if we were indeed located at the gate of hell. I didn't necessarily feel any safer knowing that this group "held the keys." But beyond that, I couldn't imagine why a tiny goddess temple in the middle of the desert would be seen as a threat to the largest religion in the United States and cause otherwise normal middle-aged Arizonans to dress up in torn sheets and chant.

Making the Circle

The public nature of the rituals is not only in line with the temple's philosophical stance but truly a thing of chaotic beauty. As a priestess, I gained valuable experience fielding questions and reactions on the spot from a widely varied set of participants. I crafted ceremonies to be accessible to the newcomer, each with the richness and beauty of the goddess tradition.

"The circle shapes us, body and mind. Heart and soul are one." So goes a chant commonly sung as the circle is cast at the beginning of rituals.[11] It is the circle that is the primary form of the ritual, both physically and philosophically.

Physically, the circle demarcates the area of sacred practice, forming a womb where we may safely dwell and be nourished—a place to retreat, a place to grow. On the horizontal plane, the circle connects the four directions, bringing us into harmony with the space. I imagine a circle of hearts formed, creating loving, sacred space. On the vertical plane, we connect the great cosmos

above and the rich earth below, completing the grand circle of
creation and destruction. In ritual we are shaped by the circles we
create. Our bodies and minds curve to meet and connect, and our
hearts and souls become one.

The defining ideal of the circle is the elegant single line,
perfectly rounded and seamlessly meeting. As is often the case,
the ideal and the reality are sometimes far apart, and the wide
variety of people who attended temple rituals didn't always mix
well. So instead of one simple elegant line, the reality is that this
circle is woven, like a wreath, from local materials that were
not cultivated for the purpose of being interwoven. As priestess, I tried to weave these bits of the old and brittle desert-dried
twigs with the supple and yellow-flowered creosote branches, the
thorny and hardy mesquite boughs, and the frayed cotton puffs
that blew in from afar. All of these pieces made up our desert
wreath, our sacred circle, which in reality was ovoid with bits
sticking out on the sides. But it was gritty and real, sublime in its
authentic beauty.

Even though the temple is dedicated as a goddess temple,
many Pagans who came continued to argue for and insist upon
having a male deity invoked. Peace activists took umbrage at
Sekhmet, a goddess associated with war. Other comers took
offense at the peace activist stance. Some vociferously disagreed
with the decidedly liberal political bent. Others consigned the
priestesses and rituals to the "fluffy bunny" category, totally
unsuited to serve a goddess of the strength of Sekhmet. Some
who came to support peace issues were put off by the Pagan rituals. Some who came to participate in Pagan rituals were put off
by the political activism.

But somehow, in some way, these disparate individuals
came to the temple for ceremony. And once in the circle, we
were, almost always, truly woven together. I can only ascribe

this to pure and unadulterated magick, the work of the Divine, the expert weaver who saw within all of our hearts the connecting threads. And I can only say that, as priestess, I worked so very hard to open my heart to each person who came, to meet each in perfect love and perfect trust of the structure and beauty of our desert wreath. To do this, I realized that I had to be not only sure of my purpose and strong in my stance but that I also had to see each person as an integral and necessary part of our circle. To do that, I had to be clear about myself and my intentions and I had to stay connected to the Divine.

Clarity and Open-Hearted Generosity

I realized early in my tenure as priestess that I must stay connected to the Divine to allow things to come through me instead of from me. Everything depended on that: my ability to lead ritual, my ability to stay centered, my ability to understand those who came to the temple, my ability to see my way out of difficult issues.

Striving to stay connected to the Divine made another point painfully apparent: I had to be clear, to the depths of my soul. I had to understand what I was, where my limits were, and accept totally who I was. I had to be able to be fully and totally present at each moment of ritual, wide open to everything, and firmly, firmly rooted. This was a real challenge.

After ritual, we gathered around a campfire for a potluck. On one occasion in my first few months, a young man approached me. In front of the group gathered, he critiqued the ritual, comparing it rather unfavorably to Patricia's rituals. It took a minute for me to get my wits about me because even though I knew his intention was not to maliciously embarrass me, being dressed down by a stern teenager in front of everyone was, well, embarrassing. I reached through my bare feet into the desert earth that supported me and felt a swell of support that reached my heart. I thanked the young man.

I had to know what I believed and feel my firm rootedness. I wanted to hear people with open ears and an open heart and to stay in a place of nonjudgment or nonattachment, while never wavering in my own judgment. I had to do this with strength from within, for only strength from within would allow me not to be swayed from without. My college administrative experience came in very handy here. In that role, I was accustomed to listening to multiple points of view, listening to people's issues and complaints and suggestions while still holding my own view clear, but doing my job with heart wasn't required; I just needed to be fair. Now, I needed to do it with the most genuine of natures, with the most open of hearts.

Moving from fair to genuine and open-hearted was harder than I thought. But to be an effective priestess, that was what I needed to do.

So I began to cultivate clarity and open-heartedness. I began chanting daily, to clear my lungs and my mind. I began exercising regularly, including dancing, tai chi, and chi gong. I journaled regularly to examine and embrace my personal demons. I began to see where my heart was closed, tight, unable to expand. I finally realized that fear was this band around my heart, keeping it closed. As I saw the disconnect between my fear and the open heart I yearned for, I sought out a way to face my own fears. Sekhmet, Lioness Goddess, fanned the flames of courage within. I needed to move beyond my ego, my attachment, and for this I turned to Chinnamasta.

I had begun a devotion a number of years ago to the Goddess Chinnamasta, recognized by both Hindus and Buddhists. She is one of the ten Mahavidyas that are emanations of Ma Kali, and her name means "severed head." She is represented as a woman who in one hand holds a sword and in the other hand her head, which she severed with her own sword. Three streams of blood issue from her neck: two into the mouths of the *yoginis* dancing beside her and one into her own mouth.

For me, Chinnamasta represents many of the aspects that I wanted to cultivate as a priestess. She is generous, severing her own head to quench the thirst of the *dakinis*[12] attending her. She has attained a state of nonattachment to self with the severing of her own head. I, too, wanted to attain a state of open-hearted generosity, not attached to my self, my ego. So I chanted to Sekhmet and Chinnamasta, opening myself to each of their gifts, working to cultivate clarity and open-hearted generosity.

Journeys: Healers and Warriors

I also searched for spiritual guidance through journeys. The terms *journey* or *shamanic journey*, in the context of spiritual practice, refer to an out-of-body experience in which the soul travels to another reality, often referred to as "non-ordinary reality." One method used to journey is to be supported by an asynchronous, constant drumbeat. On these journeys, the seeker often meets other beings, some of whom are guides and teachers. It was on one of these journeys that I met my maternal grandmother, who continues to be one of my guides.

My first journey was rather spectacular, and it happened in a suite at the Benson Hotel in downtown Portland, Oregon, at an American Association for Women in Community Colleges conference. I can't remember what other sessions I attended at the conference, though most likely they centered on themes such as understanding grant writing, charting one's career, and institutional leadership. But fortunately I chose to spend the afternoon in a session with Rowan Wolf, experiencing my first journey. Rowan explained the journey process and led the ritual, using a taped drumbeat for sonic support. And down the rabbit hole I went. It was a life-changing experience.

My strongest memory of that first journey was meeting a guide in the form of a snake, and becoming a snake myself. We slithered through the grass together, racing along. The sensation was potent, compelling, and very real. Afterward, as we went around the circle and some discussed their journeys, I remember bubbling over with excitement about meeting a snake and becoming a snake. I also remember the woman sitting next to me recoiling. Clearly my enthusiasm was not universally shared.

Over the next couple of decades, I kept up my personal journey practice as well as taking classes with Michael Harner and the Foundation for Shamanic Studies.[13] After moving to the environs of Las Vegas, I was lucky to have the opportunity to take classes from and study with Sylvia Brallier, a healer and priestess.[14] While at the temple, I took some remarkable journeys, with lessons and healings aplenty.

When I go into the journey, my guide is there to meet me. And then in walks a tall, beautiful woman with long blond hair and a purple robe. She shows me a scene where I see myself and two others. An ogre-man is attacking a very defenseless and small blond woman, and I am between them, in full warrior gear, wielding a rather large sword. I want to cut off the ogre's arms, but instead my purple-robed teacher shows me that I should touch him, that I should touch the fierce ogre. So I do, though I am loathe to do it. When I touch him, he changes. He is still ogre-like, but he is not aggressive. He does not want to harm the woman anymore. Another person comforts the

*woman, and the ogre-man cries on my shoulder. That is
the message for me—that to be a warrior is to be a healer,
healing the most ugly, most aggressive, most horrible.*

*I reject this message. I feel that if I take the side of the
ogres, then no one will see me as a healer; they will see
me as protecting the dangerous, siding with the enemy.
But that is part of the lesson, that there are no enemies. I
need to move to a place where I believe, truly, that there
are no enemies. It is a very powerful thing to heal an
ogre-man, and I must be very strong and brave, and very
clear with myself and my intention.*

*When I reject the idea that I should heal instead of
fight, my purple-robed teacher walks away. I call her
back, but she says that if I'm not interested in really
learning, she'd rather not waste her time. I say that the
whole idea of being a healer is not only unappealing to
me but actually frightens me.*

*Why do I feel this way? Maybe because the results of
healing are dependent on both parties, whereas the result
of a fight is dependent only on my own skill. The suc-
cessful result of a healing is dependent on the openness
of the recipient and the skill of the healer. It is truly a
cooperative effort, where the outcome may look different
from what either person expected, and it may look different from what the onlookers expect. Whereas success in a
battle, well, that's pretty clear.*

*But I call to her, asking her to return. And I say, "I
choose this life." Only then does she turn around and
walk toward me.*

*She places a ring set with a stone in my brain. I try to
see what kind of stone. I think it is an amethyst, but she
says that I am not ready to know that, and she is a little*

*irritated that I feel I need to know. She says that a snake
is part of the healing that I can use for others. And she
says that I am not ready. There is much to learn.*

After that journey, I felt dismayed, naïve, juvenile. As if,
once again, I had failed a test. Even now, as I write this section, I
know that I still fall so short of living every day with the attitude
that I have no enemies. And every time I do put someone on the
"enemy" side, I see how these lines in the sand that I have drawn
have put me on the other side, in a place where I am unable to
reach out. And that really doesn't help at all.

Women and the Goddess Temple [15]

I lecture at various academic venues on Goddess Spirituality,
and I continue to be amazed at the answer to my question: "Does
your god have a gender?" While the wording would seem to
make the question rhetorical, people almost always answer: "No,
my god does not have a gender." Given the statistic that over 75
percent of people living in the United States claim Christianity
as their faith, when I lecture I assume that most of my audience
is Christian.[16] When I ask them to describe their god, to tell me
what that god looks like in art, many times someone will mention a long white beard, which firmly answers the gender inquiry.
But even if they don't go as far as to mention a beard, when I ask
them if their god is a woman, they are shocked and absolutely,
defiantly sure that their genderless god is not a woman. We
women who create life, the highest of all divine acts, cannot be
considered a god.

Between my experiences at the temple and in academia, it
has become clear to me that most women in twenty-first-century
American culture never see themselves as divine. And it is no

wonder. The most predominant images of women in the modern media are as accoutrements to products such as cars or purses.

This to me is one of the greatest gifts of the goddess temples, because images of the Female Divine are important. They are important because they begin the process of consecrating women's bodies as divine. When we as women begin to see our bodies as a reflection of the Divine, then our bodies are removed from the sole category of "object of the male gaze" to corporealized divinity, the embodiment of the Divine.

When women come into the temple, they see themselves, and they see themselves venerated. They see themselves in various shapes and colors, from the round and almond-eyed Madre del Mundo to the black and slim Sekhmet to the brown and regal Virgen de Guadalupe. We women have lived our lives trying to see ourselves in the image of the Christian God, living with the cognitive dissonance of the sound of Charlton Heston's voice as God, in Michelangelo's beefy finger, and in the picture tacked on the wall in Sunday school of a man's aged and ageless face whose white beard melts into the clouds. We live in this culture of the image of God as white and male.

As if this were not enough to get the point across, most of those who represent God in the Christian religion—the priests, preachers, and pastors—are men. And if women do represent the Christian God, there is almost always a controversy involved. Still, we women have persevered to find ourselves in the Divine and to see ourselves as divine, and even more courageously to represent the Divine. A sigh of relief automatically escapes me and the cognitive dissonance melts away when I am in the presence of an image of the Divine that is female.

Images of the Female Divine are important because they embody the divine qualities of the feminine. The roles of mother, healer, guide, protector, lover, provider, and nurturer combine with the qualities of compassion, justice, truth, fertility, strength, and love to present women in multiple dimensions.

One afternoon while I was sitting in the temple with a small fire, a woman drove up. As she made her way to the temple, I called out so that my presence wouldn't surprise her. She came in, apologizing for bothering me. I invited her to sit with me, explaining that the temple was here for her. We sat in silence, ringed in goddesses. I fed the fire with tiny desert twigs, the crackling as background music. She looked around at each face of these Divine Females. I don't know what went through her mind, but we sat for a long time in that sweet silence, tears running down our cheeks intermittently. I rose to depart, and holding my hands in front of my heart, I bowed my head to her, in recognition of the Divine that lives within her. She bowed her head to me.

It is of course no small wonder why graven images are so tightly controlled by religious traditions.

I sit in front of the statue of Sekhmet in the temple. She is divine and human; animal and woman; power and love. Her lioness head stirs a chord inside of me that remembers when humans and animals were sisters, when we were one. Her breasts, one larger than the other, mirror my own humanity in her divinity. I am powerful, divine, and holy; I am woman. Yes, I desire more spaces and more idols of the Female Divine because it is at her feet that I find what is attained at the end of desire.

Men and the Goddess Temple

The idea of having a temple solely dedicated to the veneration of the Female Divine rankles some people. There are many Pagans who believe that a female and male deity must be honored together, just as a priestess and priest must both lead ceremony. There are many who follow Abrahamic-tradition religions that view the idea of the Divine in female form as heresy. And then, there are men who just plain feel left out if they don't see themselves represented.

While I respect the beliefs of the Pagans and Abrahamic followers, it's hard for me to muster sympathy for the third group, as divine female imagery has been severely limited in Euro-American culture. Women have made great efforts to see themselves in the male divine form; in Christianity, to find themselves in God the Father. If women have managed for the last couple of thousand years to do it, I think it is possible for men to see themselves in the Female Divine.

At the temple rituals, it was wonderful to see women and men gathered together in the circle, honoring Sekhmet, honoring the land, honoring the temple, supporting one another in their prayers, their dreams, their sorrows.

Both women and men both helped with the maintenance of the temple and the grounds, and both took different parts in the ceremonies. The priestesses led ceremonies, allowing a space where women could shine in full spiritual leadership capacity without the possibility of being overshadowed.

However, there were times when I saw an empty space. I was perplexed, and still am, about why men did not want to get together exclusively with other men. Or perhaps it was not that they didn't want to, it was just that they rarely did it. Even in our temple community, men were sometimes upset when women got together alone. They felt excluded from New Moon or other special women's rituals. My answer to that was, well, organize something, and do it. That's what we women do.

I really don't know why men don't gather more often in a

spiritual context. I personally gain so much joy and deep personal satisfaction from being with women that I don't understand why men don't desire these connections. But maybe men don't see the lack of male gatherings as an empty space, and that's why they do not try to fill it. Or maybe they do fill it in a way that is very different from the manner in which women gather with invitations, potluck dishes, and the like. What I do know is that I am in no way qualified to understand the reality of what it is to be male in today's society.

I admit there were times while I was priestess when I felt all of the rituals should be exclusively for women. One incident particularly troubled me. During one gathering, I had arranged the ritual in the evening to have a women's dancing circle, a men's dancing circle, and then a full circle with us all together. While the men were dancing in their circle, saying what they were grateful for, one man shouted, "uncomplicated women." He was met with resounding cheers from the circle of dancers. And no man refuted his claim. It was disheartening and disappointing for me. Not so much that this young man had said this, but that no other man countered by expressing gratitude for "complex women."

By the next Full Moon ceremony, I was seriously contemplating what I would have to do to make all of the rituals women-only. As I walked up the path from my house to the temple, my head was spinning with thoughts of whether the rituals would be richer—and easier—with only women participating. On the way I was met by two men who had brought their young daughters to the ritual. Both of these men, regulars at temple ceremonies, were devoted fathers, and to see the love and joy they shared with their daughters filled my heart. One of the fathers had brought drums, and he and his eight-year-old daughter played together. He patiently taught her a rhythm, and she quickly followed his lead. The other father held his daughter, around one

year old, on his hip throughout the entire ceremony, and she laid
her head on his chest when she grew tired.

I thought about how these men cared for their daughters,
supported them, encouraged them, and taught them. It seemed
to me that truly these men must see themselves in the face of
the Divine Female, without emasculation, without fear, and with
unconditional love, and I wondered if they found solace in her
image. I opened to a profound beauty, healing, and joy in mixed
rituals.

Priestesses: On Creating the Circle of Sisters

During the first couple of years, I prepared and led almost every
ritual, which meant at least one ritual every other week. It was
the best priestess education I could have had. I began to understand the seasonal cycles, the psychic underlay, what worked and
didn't work in ritual. I began to understand the different threads
that wove through the temple: Sekhmet, feminism, peace activism, principles of the Gift Economy, the philosophical stances of
the founder and the former priestesses, as well as the Euro-Pagan
traditions and Native American traditions that arose from the
people who attended and from the land itself.

Taking all of this into account, I saw that the temple needed
a lineage of women beyond the temple priestess, a lineage that
would carry the information and philosophy beyond my tenure
there, a group of women who would form the links of the chain
that would stretch across time. So I began the first steps of creating a circle of priestesses. As always, the first steps required
coming to terms with myself.

If I brought priestesses on board, they would need to be
initiated. I would have to be the person to do the initiation. That
frightened me. I had never actually done an initiation or been

initiated by anyone other than myself. I hadn't studied in any
lineage. I had read, practiced, and done my own thing, with a
variety of teachers along my way, but I had no higher authority
or higher recognized power to endow me with anything that I
could possibly pass along. I felt as if I hadn't done enough, didn't
know enough, and didn't have any authority to initiate others.

But, if I didn't do it, who would? Would someone else come
in and initiate priestesses for me? Did I even want someone else
to? I had to move beyond the chattering of my mind that told me I
wasn't good enough to do this.

Then there was the question of hubris. There was a certain
amount of presumption involved in calling myself a priestess. But
it was one thing to finally get accustomed to being called a priestess and another thing entirely to deem myself worthy of naming
others as priestesses. And yet another thing to initiate them. I
have always eschewed the title "High Priestess" as it asserts a
spiritual hierarchy. Instead I took the title "Temple Priestess" to
designate that I was the one who lived at the temple. Nevertheless, by initiating priestesses, I felt that I was raising myself above
others, and that felt awkward as well.

At this juncture I knew I just had to get to the point of believing enough in myself, without any outside legitimizing authority,
because if I didn't initiate priestesses, if I didn't do my piece in
bringing about the recognition of women's spiritual leadership,
who would? I asked five women who were regulars to the temple,
women who had already shown themselves as priestesses, leading
parts of the rituals, planning, setting up, and otherwise helping.
I began with Candace Novaembre, who had been involved with
the temple for years. Then I chose Dot, Jen, and Lily. Their many
hats included teachers, professors, small business owners, office
managers, nurses, and artists. They were women of accomplish-
ment who dedicated their time to creating a spiritual community.

At our initiation ceremony, we placed necklaces that we had ceremonially beaded around one another's necks, in an act of initiating one another. That, finally, felt right.

In that manner, we started a sisterhood of priestesses.

As sisters, we are one another's truth tellers. We are one another's loving and honest mirrors. We advise, even when we are not queried. And we let go so that each may fly on her own wings. Our sisters are our bonds with the deepest mysteries. As sisters, we are the ones who bleed, we are the ones who birth, we are the ones who nourish, we are the ones who weave the web, and we are the ones who cut the cord. As women, as sisters, as priestesses, we stand at the doorways of life and death, bonded by the cycles of our bodies and our lives.

Feeling Alone in the Circle

Throughout my three years at the temple, my feelings of inclusivity ebbed and flowed. In my first few months at the temple, I was greeted lovingly by a number of people. Gifts floated in, notes of welcome came in the mail, and calls of greeting all made me feel at home.

I later realized that one of the saving graces of coming into this position from the outside was that by not knowing anyone beforehand, I did not feel betrayed by those who had regularly come to temple rituals before but didn't any longer. Soon enough, though, people began showing up regularly and becoming a part of things and a new circle was formed.

The painful moments occurred sparingly, but continually, over the three years I was there. Out of the blue, people I had never met before would approach me and say that the temple means a great deal to them and had been very important to them for years and years. I couldn't help it; hearing these words struck deep at my heart because many of these people lived nearby, in Las Vegas, and yet after I arrived they had never come by to greet me, welcome me, or offer help.

That feeling of pain slowly turned to a feeling of betrayal. And then, to make matters worse, people would meet me and tell me that they used to come to the temple for years when Patricia was priestess. They would wax poetically about how the land and Patricia had meant so much to them, and that they just hadn't been able to make it out here in the last two years. And of course, they often added that it had nothing to do with me, personally.

My heart would become so very heavy. I could not fight back the feelings of betrayal. My thoughts would run evil little word circles like this: If this temple and this land meant so much to you, how could you not even have come out to meet me, introduce yourself, gather a group to come and bring some cookies and say hello in those first few months, invite me to dinner in Las Vegas—anything? It was then that I knew I was getting into serious internal trouble; time for intervention.

I went inward to talk to the part of me that felt betrayed and hurt. I brought myself to the place of recognition that this was my path, this path as priestess, and that I was here to walk it. If the old circle had not dispersed, the new circle could not have been woven. It was a lovely new circle and I wouldn't change a thing.

But, beyond my better judgment, I continued to feel hurt and betrayed. When I had begun my spiritual path in earnest, I learned from a beautiful woman named Stardancer. One of my most prized gifts from her is a silver pendant of a woman shrouded in a cloak. When she gave it to me, Stardancer told me that this path was one that I would walk alone. And she was right.

I wished I had kept up with Stardancer, but I hadn't. Perhaps

one day she will read these words and be amazed that she had
such a great effect on my life, yet I did not stay connected with
her. I wonder if she would feel betrayed by me?

What was it about this job, about being priestess, that
brought on these feelings of isolation? I remember the morning
that I received the call informing me that Patricia had died. I suddenly felt the entirety of the temple and its heritage fall squarely
on my shoulders. I had no idea she had been carrying so much of
the burden, but it was true. And at that moment, I really was all
alone.

At first, I thought this feeling of loneliness was a lack of
other priestesses. Certainly, when I brought on other priestesses
and we formed our sisterhood, some of the weight on my shoulders was lessened. But I was still alone. Was it the loneliness of
living out in the remote desert? I didn't really think that was it.
Ben and I led a paradisiacal life together, sharing every sunrise
and sunset, enjoying every breath. And I had lots of friends and
some very good friends; I never felt friendless. Was the loneliness due to the fact that I live in a culture that hardly recognizes
female spiritual authority? That my experience, my work, and my
calling were practically invisible?

For whatever reason, I did feel alone. And at those moments,
I would put on the pendant from Stardancer. And even though it
did not make me feel less alone, it made me feel better somehow
about being alone.

Initiation and Personal Evolution

A fter my first year, I felt that I had the job duties down. Plan and lead the rituals—check. Keep the website up-to-date and monitor chat group—check. Keep the guest house clean and organized; coordinate guest arrivals/departures—check. Clean the temple and take care of offerings—check. Answer e-mail and phone inquiries, even the weird ones—check. Can tell the history of the temple and the story of Sekhmet at a moment's notice—check. But though I had the daily tasks down, I still did not fully feel like a priestess.

The Parameters of Mind and Profession

I had not realized how identified I was with my profession as a college administrator and faculty member. When the question, "So, what do you do?" inevitably came up, I would sometimes claim my position as adjunct faculty at the College of Southern Nevada as my primary profession. When I first started at the temple, I told some of my acquaintances that I was moving to Nevada to manage a retreat center. I think that's probably the story I first told my mother.

When asked the "What do you do?" question, and when I

didn't skirt the issue and instead replied, "I am a priestess for a goddess temple," I received varied reactions. Sometimes the subject was changed immediately to safer territory. Anything is safer than contemplating the profession of a priestess. Infrequently, though, when I told people that I was a priestess, they wanted to know more. Some were fascinated that I lived in the desert; they wanted to know about the temple, about Sekhmet, and what my daily life was like. Between sessions at an academic conference, in the safety of the women's washroom, I confided my true source of employment to one of the presenters, an anthropologist whose work I greatly admired. She kindly advised me that I should not tell others. There is a strong anti-religious bias in academia. Researching religion is an acceptable course of study, but fervently practicing a religion, believing in religion—well, that is tantamount to drinking the Kool-Aid.

On rare occasions, my title of priestess brought absurdly lewd images to others' minds. In one bizarre three-month period during my second year, I received a few phone calls from men who wanted to be dominated by a priestess, who wanted to serve the goddess through self-abasement. I explained kindly but firmly that subjugation was anathema to honoring the goddess. I never answered the letter from the inmate in Kentucky who sought absolution through subjugation.

After the first year, I became more comfortable with my title of Priestess. I am especially grateful that Genevieve insisted that this was my job title, because I don't know if I would have taken up the mantle on my own. In the back of my mind, I still saw myself as a college administrator; I could feel the parameters, the box of that profession, as visceral walls. After the first year, I knew that to move ahead, to be effective, I had to step into my power as a priestess, completely and totally. I had to rid my mind of the continual message that I was a fraud.

When I reflect on my mental state regarding the profession of priestessing at the time, it is no wonder that I felt this way. There isn't a lot of support for being a priestess, and it certainly isn't something twenty-first-century America encourages as a viable or honorable or serious vocation. It's no wonder I thought myself a fraud; everyone else thought of the profession of priestess as fraudulent. And probably some people thought of me personally as a fraud. I found out that some of these people weren't afraid to test that assumption in public.

One bright April morning, I woke up very early, pushed contacts into my sleepy eyes, and put on my infrequently worn navy suit and pumps, with some large silver artisan earrings to spice up the look. Fueled with a steaming travel mug of green tea, I started the three-hour drive from Cactus Springs to Cedar City, Utah. I had been invited to give a presentation on women's spirituality at the Southern Utah University Women's Conference. I was introduced with all my credentials: Anne Key, PhD in Women's Spirituality and Priestess of the Temple of Goddess Spirituality Dedicated to Sekhmet. It was something to hear it all out loud.

At the end of the presentation came questions. The first few were easily answered and dealt with the material I had presented. Then a young, red-haired woman stood up and in a strong voice full of challenge with a clearly perceptible edge of sarcasm, she asked, "What makes you think you are a priestess?"

Good question.

My answer? Something like, "It is the title given to me on my job description. Just as the title 'director' was on my last job description." Not a heartfelt answer, but it wasn't a heartfelt question either.

And it wasn't just that I thought myself a fraud, I began wondering why I kept thinking I was a fraud. I had never thought of myself as a fraud when I was a college faculty member or administrator. In fact, no one had ever said, "What makes you think you are a department director?" But there is no universally recognized governing body that designates priestesses. In many religious institutions there is little recognition for women's leadership. In fact, most religions do not even ordain women. So, a priestess of a goddess temple? I could not depend on outside help for strength and respect in this role. My convictions and assurance had to come from within, from a deep place of honesty and strength that would be unwavering in the face of near universal distrust and disbelief.

After my first year at the temple, I decided I needed to move beyond what I was and move into what I had become. To do that, I privately but formally recognized my status and my title as priestess with an initiation ritual.

Initiation: The Severing of the Head

There are certainly a number of books outlining group and self-initiations, but I had not attended many initiations. In fact, the only one I could remember was my own initiation into a goddess-based spiritual path. On one rainy evening in Portland on Imbolc 1992, the first day of spring, four of us devised our own initiation and dedicated ourselves in service to the goddess.

As priestess of the temple, I truly wished to have someone else initiate me, but that was not presenting itself as a possibility. Patricia was not only ill but working through her own process of having left her post as priestess of the temple that she had held for ten years. In a year I had certainly made friends, but I did not have many in a close, trusted, shared-mind type of circle. I wanted to open myself fully to this initiation, so I wanted to be sure that those in attendance were clear and unambiguous in their "midwifery" of me in this situation. I chose two of my closest friends, Ben, who was by now my husband, and my friend and fellow priestess, Sylvia Brallier.

My devotion to Chinnamasta had led me to a sense of clarity and service, a sense that when I moved beyond my ego's needs, the spirit of life would flow. I wanted to do something visceral to honor the cutting off of my own head, the symbolic removal of my ego. What did I have to give, what part of me embodied my ego? The answer was obvious: my hair.

I loved my long hair. It was full, curly, and sexy. When I danced, it danced with me. People knew me and remembered me because of my hair. Even if I didn't always feel good about my body image, I could count on my hair. My hair made me feel good in a conventional way; it made me feel beautiful in a very mainstream manner, a feeling that hasn't come to me a lot in this life. My hair was a big part of my identity. In a similar fashion, my job was part of my identity. While my hair gave me a conventional, female identity, my job gave me a professional identity.

I fell back on my administrative identity. It helped me in many ways—organizing rituals, solving conflicts between people, creating a sense of mission, motivation. But, like all things that are helpful, my administrative persona also brought with it limits. I was an administrator leading a temple, and I wanted to be, needed to be, a priestess leading this temple. I needed to break out of my former self—or rather, I needed to expand myself.

That was when I decided to include shaving my head in my initiation as priestess. I had to leave everything behind and move forward. Otherwise I would be ineffective at best. And I so much wanted to be good at the job. The real heart of the matter was that I had to get real and be real. I had to be crystal clear. To be a good priestess, a competent priestess, I had to be my most honest self. I had to get my own stuff out of the way: my fears of being called a freak, my fears of others misunderstanding me, my fears of what people would think.

It was a sunny and beautiful autumn afternoon on October 3, 2005, with a new moon and the annular solar eclipse for extra energy for this new beginning. Ben, Sylvia, and I met at the temple. Sylvia arrived beautifully arrayed in a white skirt and flowing top. Frankincense trailed out of the censer and wafted around us and up through the roof. We cleansed by smudging, fanning the smoke from the censer over us to purify and ready ourselves for ceremony. The love and kindness perceptibly welling from Sylvia's heart buoyed me: yes, this was the right course. I lit the fire and the dry twigs crackled and then caught, a bright yellow-orange flame dancing between the brambles, heat embracing us all. Sylvia pulled up a pillow and readied to play her tamboura and recite Chinnamasta's 108 names. Ben gathered his tools: scissors and battery-operated beard trimmer. Sylvia and I began by chanting to Sekhmet. I spoke her sacred names and asked for her guidance. Then we began the symbolic severing of my ego. As Sylvia plucked the tamboura and spoke the 108 names of Chinnamasta, Ben cut my hair.

Snip, snip, snip. Locks of hair falling over my lap, covering the ground. No second thoughts. No fear. I feel lighter. As each long hank falls, I become lighter and lighter. By the time Ben uses the electric shaver, I am giggly, effervescent. I breathe in as though I am a crystal vessel, and I exhale laughter and joy. I am free.

Initiation: The Demarcation

It might be thought that shaving one's head is a definitive statement. However, I decided that I wanted my initiation to be immutable, visceral, and affirming. I wanted it to be a "no turning back" sort of event. I wanted it to mark this moment for me forever. I wasn't just choosing this path of priestess for however long my tenure in this job lasted; I was choosing this path for life. So this initiation needed to bring me clarity and a clear turning from my past. Not a break, but a turn. And it needed to have a lasting, indelible mark, a source of reminder and a source of power.

A tattoo was in order.

As I was initiating as her priestess, I wanted Sekhmet to decide where I should place the tattoo, so I journeyed to her. She met me immediately, and I posed my question. She took my left forearm and raked her giant claws over it. My flesh shredded down to the bone. She then raised her mighty paw, with claws extended, and again raked down to the bone. But this time, flesh appeared under her claws, and my arm was formed anew, ready for a tattoo.

For the design, I wanted a constellation in honor of the stars that had taught me so much. From early summer to late autumn, the Milky Way is visible as it crawls away from the Las Vegas glare. The tail of Scorpio curves elegantly across the horizon, crossing the bottom of the Milky Way, and Libra extends from Scorpio's head. From the temple, Scorpio and Libra are the superstar celebrities of the southern summer sky's nightly astrological movie, and each features prominently in my own astral chart.

Early star-watchers, including the Greeks, considered what we now call Libra to be part of the constellation Scorpio. Libra formed the claws of the great scorpion. Some three thousand years ago, the beginning of fall equinox was marked by the sun entering Libra, when light and dark throughout the world was in balance. The claws of Scorpio have long been associated with balance, apportionment.

For the ancient Egyptians, the scorpion was a symbol of

motherhood, associated with the marriage bed. Scorpion mothers carry their young on their backs and are protective of them. Like many venomous creatures, scorpions are the source of the cures to their poison. The best antidote to scorpion venom is antivenom from the scorpion. Thus, death and life, pain and relief, are all part of her.

The Romans divided the constellations of Scorpio and Libra, leaving Scorpio with her stinging tail and severing her from her power to balance, separating these twinned forces and weakening each. The Romans allied the Libran power of balance with the government, the state. For many feminists, this is clearly one of those moments where the auspices of women—as those who give birth, who midwife the dead, who hold the power of life in balance—were taken from their cultural, and some would say natural, place and eclipsed by the state, the government, a body which eschewed the participation of women.

One afternoon soon after, I sat with a sacred tattoo artist. He listened to my story of the constellations, my personal vows to unite these constellations again, to unite the wholeness of myself as a woman with the cycle of life and death and with the power of balance. He picked his ink color carefully, mixing a blend the color of my freckles. Serendipitously, three of my fellow priestesses were there as well, including Sylvia. They toned and chanted during the tattoo, honoring my path and lending me strength and love.

Ever since, my arm has felt as if it glows. I feel the stars shine through my skin just as they do in the sky, their magick geometry pervading my work, my thoughts, my senses, my direction. My initiation was complete.

Spinning the Wheel:
The Rituals of the Year

The temple ritual calendar comprises both solar and lunar ritual days. The solar rituals, eight per year, follow what is commonly referred to as "The Wheel of the Year." This calendar is based on the annual solar cycle of two equinoxes, two solstices, and four cross-quarter days. This calendar is somewhat based on pre-Christian Celtic practices, but the form in which it is presently practiced by many modern Pagans is mostly based on twentieth- and twenty-first-century derivations.[17] These eight solar ritual days align me with the extremes and balances of the Earth; by celebrating them I too turn with the wheel.

Leading ritual through every season and every moon phase, I began to see how the rituals engaged me with the land. My internal workings began to follow new and different cues. Of course, I had always noted such obvious differences as the length of daylight and night, the budding and flowering of plants, the falling of the leaves. But now, I began to notice these happenings sooner, and their details held my attention throughout their whole cycle. Instead of suddenly noticing the new green leaves on the trees in spring, I noticed when the cottonwoods set bud and how their leaves unfolded like butterfly wings from a cocoon. I had time to notice these things. As well, being intricately woven into the land and the seasons was now a part of my job.

The Seasonal Dance of Light and Dark

I had always thought of the seasons in terms of temperature;
summer is hot and winter is cold. But after following the seasonal rituals for a year, I began to understand the seasons in terms of
light, as befits a solar calendar. The solstices are at the extremes,
the lightest and the darkest days. The equinoxes are the balances,
almost equal light for day and night. So the year goes from
extreme to balance to extreme to balance. While the northern
hemisphere is at one extreme, the southern hemisphere is at the
other. On December 21, the northern hemisphere is at the winter
solstice and the southern hemisphere is at the summer solstice.
But the world meets again at the balance points of the equinoxes.
I began to feel the global undulation of the waxing and waning
of the solar year, the dance of light and dark.

In the solar year, the solstices and equinoxes mark the
height of each season while the cross-quarter days are the
moments of change, the beginning of each season. In this way,
the season of winter begins at Samhain (known more popularly
as Hallowe'en), which is the cross-quarter day between the fall
equinox and winter solstice. Winter solstice is the height of the
season of winter, so we can also call it midwinter, just as we
might refer to the summer solstice as midsummer, reminiscent of
William Shakespeare's play.

I moved each year through the 365-day pattern of dark
and light, through the extreme and the balance. The short lunar
cycles compressed the cycle of light and dark into twenty-nine
days. I began each lunar cycle with the new moon, felt its tide
peak at the full moon, and then started again at new. I was
finally living a life connected to the Earth, the sun, and the
moon. And to lead rituals through each of these cycles, I had to
immerse myself, connect myself completely to them.

I not only wanted to live these cycles, I wanted to embody them so fully that I could confidently lead others through them. In my pursuit of personal clarity, I used the winter rituals to explore within myself. Just like cleaning under the bed, I found things I did not want to find. The first winter was consumed with discovering my feeling of inadequacy and that I was not supported by the temple community; both feelings were baseless in reality. I spent my second winter examining reality and ego gratification: what did I need to be assured of, and why did I need those assurances? I used the spring rituals to nurture little seedlings within, such as my desire to be open-hearted to everyone who came to the temple and to be able to have a genuine empathy for each person, no matter how they irritated me. I used summer to be expressive and ecstatic, to dance for joy and lead others in dance and song. I used autumn to let go of my own dry leaves to allow room for buds the next spring. The dry leaves I shook off that second year were my fears of ridicule.

After living this life for a while, it was hard for me to remember that everyone else lived the way I used to live, following a calendar directed by work or American culture. I began to understand that the people who came to the temple for rituals were looking for this connection, this experience, this breath of a different life. Even though their experience was sandwiched between work and sleep, the rituals compelled us all to become conscious and connected with the Earth and sky, the solar and lunar cycles.

Full Moon Meanings

The temple ritual calendar includes lunar festivals. Each full moon is celebrated with a ritual and each new moon is celebrated with a ritual exclusively for women. So each month there were two rituals in the lunar cycle, full and new. Every six weeks brought a solar cycle ritual, a solstice, an equinox, or a cross-quarter day.

I quickly realized the importance of the celestial cycles and ritual, and just as quickly knew that I was out of my area of expertise. What did a "full moon" really mean? How did the solar and lunar cycles influence each other? How did the astrological signs influence the solar and lunar cycles? I wanted to design rituals based on what was happening at the temple, not relying on the vagaries of information I found on Internet sites. I needed an expert. I called on Kalli Rose Halvorson—astrologer, feminist, and goddess devotee. She became the temple astrologer, calculating the exact dates and times for all the solar and lunar rituals.

Before working with Kalli, I considered all full moons to be the same—a time of heightened outward energy and a propitious moment to ask for blessings. After working with her, my ideas expanded to include the astrological influences. She also outlined the cosmic view of each ritual day in its unique holistic aspects.

I saw that each full moon was different; each solar and lunar ritual was affected by multiple influences. Understanding these influences helped me craft effective rituals that rode on the cosmic current.

The Priestess Readies for Ritual

My primary objective with each ritual was to give each person the opportunity to connect to the Divine. Most people's lives, driven by the secular and mundane, have few moments dedicated to spiritual practice. I wanted to give them the opportunity to connect, to reconnect, with the Divine within and without.

Preparing for ritual was a three-layer process. The first layer

was the planning, which would often begin a few days beforehand, especially if others were helping with the ritual. Referring
to Kalli Rose's yearly forecast, I would pick out a major theme.
For the full moon on Tuesday, March 14th, 2006, she wrote:

> Biannual lunar eclipse. Bubbling creative ferment seems
> to be accompanied by a mysterious sense of restraint,
> owing to the current retrogrades of Mercury, Jupiter, and
> Saturn and today's lunar eclipse. The release of past rela-
> tionships, jobs, homes, dreams, and projects may still be
> an important healing theme, owing to the lunar eclipse as
> well as the nurturing centrality of Ceres in the continuing
> mystic rectangle between Saturn, the Nodes, and Chiron.
> Acknowledge any mistakes made during the past year;
> honor the burning of karma; and offer up any obstacles
> to a more enlightened source. Extract the essence of
> this winter's work, and prepare to publicly share its next
> distillation in April. Use mental capabilities wisely, and
> bind any threads of the wavering mind together with
> careful practices like meditation, chant, mantra, dance,
> or song. Over the long haul, the soulful objectives and
> wider visibility of female leaders, and of female-centered
> partnerships, teachings, and organizations—as univer-
> sal expressions that uplift all beings and expressions of
> nature—are prominent features of this lunation, with
> the solar-lunar axis transmitting the Lioness and Bearess
> stars, and with a grand square involving Juno, Pluto,
> and the Nodes. Moreover, humanitarian and future-
> oriented trends in education, law, spirituality, medicine,
> and research leap into prominence with the exact square
> between Jupiter and Neptune.

Full Moon Ritual Ideas: Retire in a relaxed domestic sphere or in comfort elsewhere. Court happiness simply, raising a toast alone, or in the company of partners or friends. Social and professional identity may be mutating for many, considering the immense birthing activity currently activated by the Lioness and Bearess stars. Let go! Other celebratory suggestions: attune to Fish, Horse, Lion, Bear, and Serpent, including their deities, stars, and habitats on Earth and elsewhere. Jai Mahavidyas Kali, Tara, Sodasi, Dhumavati, Matangi.[18]

What a reminder that the idea of the full moon being about outward integration could take many forms—whether raucous or contemplative. Reading this, I gathered ideas for what the cosmic current of this full moon would be. I took the ideas of release, especially release of past mistakes and honoring the burning of karma. I also wanted to work in the ideas of "offering any obstacles up to a more enlightened source" and "extracting the essence of this winter's work."

The next step was to take these abstract concepts and bring them into the concrete. How could I create a ritual in which people could experience release, literally embody release and offering? My thoughts went to the white and green skeins of clay that weave throughout the landscape around the temple. Clay is excellent for extraction and release, and combined with the water from the Temple Spring, it is a powerful ritual tool. I thought of bringing in clay and bowls of water, having people put clay on their hands to extract obstacles. After the clay dried, they could wash their hands in bowls of water from the spring, releasing their obstacles to a more enlightened source, Mother Earth. One distinct advantage of being in an outdoor temple with a stone and earth floor is that we could do these types of rituals, messy and lovely. I began writing out the ritual, asking the priestesses and others in our temple circle if they would take a role, such as calling directions, handing out towels, filling water, invoking Sekhmet, leading a song.

The second layer of preparation involved the logistics of preparing for the ritual. The day of the ritual, Ben stocked the firewood and filled the torches with fuel, the latter being a task I absolutely loathed and loved him even more deeply for doing. For almost every ritual I made a pot of vegetarian soup, a tradition handed down from Patricia. For this particular ritual, I gathered large bowls, pitchers, and towels.

Obtaining the clay and water was an important part of the ritual preparation. In the ritual, we would ask clay to help us truly let go of obstacles, and we would ask water to cleanse us, release us. I wanted to honor their role by gathering them in a sacred and reverential manner. A few days before the ritual, Ben led me to his favorite skeins of clay. I brought an offering of my hair, thanking the earth for providing the clay that would help us transform ourselves. The morning of the ritual, I sang to the spring, thanking it for providing water for the plants, the animals, and for us. I asked water to help us that night, to wash away what doesn't serve us and to offer it to Mother Earth. My final task was to make an offering for the ritual fire. I gathered a bundle of dried lavender, grown by a friend in Oregon, and tied a red cotton cord around it. When I threw this on the fire, the scent would fill the temple, sweetening our thoughts and prayers.

The third layer of ritual preparation was highly personal. After writing the ritual and gathering the tools, I prepared myself. I wanted to be open, centered, grounded, and loving. Early that morning I went to the temple, greeting the sun. I made a small fire and sat in front of Sekhmet, opening myself to her,

asking for clarity and strength. I followed a ritual clearing exer-
cise that Sylvia had taught me, drawing love and energy from
the Earth through my whole body. I chanted to Chinnamasta and
Sekhmet for release of my ego and strength of my heart. Then
the flurry of the day ensued, full of writing e-mails, making
soup, and trotting back and forth on the dusty path to the temple.

People would arrive for ritual at around 7:00 p.m., and we
would begin at 7:30. At 5:30, I again began the process of preparing myself. I laid out my clothes for the evening, a red dress
that I had made to wear at ritual, a sturdy poly-cotton blend that
washed well. Opening the drawer the held my jewelry, I took out
my necklace with the gold visage of Sekhmet, the necklace that
all priestesses wore. I chose a small silver ring of entwined serpents and another of a seashell, in honor of the Earth and water
in our ritual tonight.

Next I headed for the shower. This was truly my time to
cleanse and release, preparing myself to lead the ceremony.
Standing under the water, I opened to its cleansing, for this water
in my shower was pumped from the same aquifer that filled
the spring. I thanked water for cleansing me and for cleansing
everyone tonight. I picked up the soap that Lily, one of the priestesses, had made and lathered it across my chest, across my heart,
cleansing and clearing myself.

This was no ordinary soap. One of the many gifts Lily
brought as a priestess was her ability to reach back to her
Mormon roots of radical self-sufficiency and rework them in a
modern Pagan context. She showed up one time at the temple
for a women's gathering, carrying baskets of soap molded in the
shape of what is often referred to as the Nile Goddess, a figure of
a woman with her arms stretched out and curved overhead.

These beautiful magickal bars led us to the idea of making
soap in a ritual setting at the temple. That idea led us to work out

how to use the ash from the temple fire to make the lye, a basic ingredient in soap making. Ben stepped in at this point, and he and Lily worked out the science of the lye. Then we made soap together at the temple in one New Moon ritual, women crowded around a cauldron over a fire. Lily led us through the process, her long hair stacked on top of her head and her plain muslin apron in stark contrast to the exquisite images on her arms: the tarot cards of The Empress, High Priestess, Magician, and Three of Swords on her right arm, and Isis, Sekhmet, Hathor, and Bast on her left. She was a frontier woman in a thoroughly modern body.

After considerable tweaking, the soap finally set. This soap is the one I used to prepare myself before ritual. Even now, when I take the soap out of its container and lather it on my heart, I feel myself open, cleansed, free.

My last step of cleansing before ritual was to brush my teeth. Before any ritual, even before chanting in the early morning, I began by brushing my teeth. I wanted my breath to be as sweet and clean as my prayers.

Clear and clean, I anointed myself with a scented oil specifically formulated for clarity and mixed by Katlyn Breene, a fellow priestess from Las Vegas.[19] I touched the chakra points on the top of my head, my third eye, and my throat to connect with the Divine in thought, perception, and speech.

I gathered my basket of ritual tools, including the smudge for the evening—copal, a tree resin—and headed down the dusty path to the temple. A car door slamming shut in the distance told me that already people were arriving. The familiar pre-ritual anxiety bubbled up within me. Was I ready? Did I have everything? Would this work? I breathed again into the desert earth below my feet, opening to the support of this sacred land. The bubbles subsided and a smile stretched across my face.

Rituals: Full Moon Release

The sun-warmed air of the day had completely dissipated by the
time we gathered for ritual, coolness seeping in with the darkness. The moon was almost overhead as we gathered outside the
temple, twenty or so souls. I introduced the night's ritual:

Tonight we are going to release fears, worries, and obstacles. Water and earth will be the elements that will aid us.
Enter the space; enter the ritual with open mind, heart,
and body. I welcome you.

Jen was there to priestess that evening. She had the smudge
ready, copal billowing out of the censer in beautiful white
clouds. We circled inside the temple. I breathed in, pulling my
breath from beneath my feet, from the earth through the stone
floor of the temple, grounding myself in the space. We called
ourselves in, a beautiful tradition from Patricia. Each person
said their name aloud, and the group repeated it three times. We
called in the directions, honoring their gifts and asking for support in our ritual. We invoked Sekhmet, chanting her mantra *Sa
Sekhem Sahu*. The priestesses helped me pass around bowls of
clay and water as I introduced the ritual:

This clay is from the sacred land here at the temple; this
water is from our sacred spring. Take a pinch of clay and
mix it with the water. Form it. Change it. Let it cover your
skin. Spend these few moments considering obstacles in
your way of achieving your highest good. What are those
obstacles? Acknowledge your mistakes. What were they?
Honor that this is your path, that all the mistakes, all the

obstacles, are truly sacred and part of your path. What
do you want to give up? Clay soaks poisons through our
pores. What do you want this clay to soak out of you?
What doesn't serve you? What is hindering you? Allow
the clay to soak this from you—release it to the clay.

We sat in silence on the cooling stones of the temple floor;
the fire crackled a bit louder. I felt the clay harden on my hand,
and I contemplated this past winter. The mistakes came flooding
in and the obstacles surmounted. My ego, slighted by the rejec-
tion of my article for a magazine, urged vengeful words from my
tongue. I had gained weight, and I felt unattractive and sloppy. I
had organized a peace event, and only three people came to the
ritual. I opened to the clay, letting it pull all of these pieces from
me. I looked at my hands, trying desperately to truly acknowledge that these character defects and mistakes were sacred. I
reached deep through the temple floor, to the deep dark earth,
seeking comfort. A literal groundswell of love moved through
me, and I saw the clay in my hands through the eyes of beauty,
through the eyes of love. I held my hands tight, honoring all the
pieces of me.

I looked up, realizing I needed to return to my position of
leading the ceremony. My voice edged into the silence of the
circle:

Turn to the person next to you. Show them your hands.
Either out loud or silently, say what you are releasing.
When you are finished, say, "I have released." Your part-
ner is to say, "It is released."

I turned to the person next to me, Jen, looked into her eyes,
and recounted my litany of mistakes. When I came to the words

"I have released," I exhaled deeply. The loving words from Jen, "It is released," sealed the moment. I opened my heart even further, loving this woman's litany of mistakes and reproaches, loving her humanity as I loved my own.

Jen moved to sit at Sekhmet's side, her brown hair reflecting the shine of the firelight. I picked up a pitcher of spring water and washed her hands at Sekhmet's feet, releasing the clay laden with the mistakes of winter, offering them to Sekhmet. Jen sighed with release and looked in my eyes, saying, "I am clear." I held her hands, feeling the clarity of life anew, and answered with "Blessed be." Then Jen took the pitcher and I opened to the sacred water pouring over my hands, the chill making the moment even more potent. I looked up at Sekhmet, opening myself even more to the cleansing and healing waters. "I am clear." I heard Jen say, "Blessed be," and I was made anew. We turned, sat on either side of Sekhmet, and washed the hands of all of those at the ritual. The water splashed on the stone, clay seeped into the ground, and we rejoiced at the releasing and clearing in the light of the full moon.

Rituals: The First Day of Spring

The first day of spring arrives at the beginning of February. In the modern Pagan tradition, this festival is commonly called *Imbolc* (spelled either *Imbolc* or *Imbolg*, and pronounced *imolk*, from the Gaelic, meaning "in the belly"), and is traditionally celebrated either on February 2nd or on the eve before. This festival is also referred to as Candlemas, originating from the Church of England. The first day of spring may be calculated as the date the sun is at 15° Aquarius, which would fall around February 3rd to 4th at the temple.

On a beautiful, chilly February night at the cross of the

quarters, about forty warmly clad people gathered in front of the temple, the area illuminated by shimmering moonlight. None of the torches were lit; the fires were dark. The inside of the temple was still festooned with the vestiges of the Winter Solstice ritual—cedar and fir boughs, pine cones, and juniper branches with their diminutive blue berries—all around the fire pit and the altars. As we stood in a circle outside the temple in the chill air, I could tell that everyone there wished I would start the fire soon. But first, I wanted to be in the dark, breathe in the dark, be enveloped by the dark. I spoke into the chill of the night:

This is the day when winter passes and spring emerges, the days grow perceptibly longer, and we begin to notice the light. This is the moment to celebrate the turn of the season, and we greet the life-bringing light. Can you sense something impending in your life? Is there something that is yet to manifest above ground into physical reality yet lies there quietly sprouting under the dark blanket of earth inside you? Plan how you will protect and nurture the new part of you that is quickening inside. As the light returns, we see the end of the long nights of winter and turn from the inner world to the outer. The Earth awakens; we awaken. Spend a moment in appreciation of your surrender to the cycles of life and of your trust that pushes the new growth forward, even when all seems cold and barren.

We smudged with a wintry blend and entered the temple. Everyone bumped around in the dark and I knew they really wished we'd light the fire. But not yet.

"Open our feet to the ground; open our heads to the cosmos; we open to the coming of the light. Feel the Earth awakening.

Feel ourselves awakening as we greet the light, the light of spring." We honored Sekhmet, Goddess of the Sun, chanting to her at the spark of the match. The tiny flame stayed hidden under the blanket of tinder. Then, in that moment when I wondered if it had really lit, the tiny spark took and the flame gave a jump for joy and leaped into the air. Light spread throughout the temple, and we were heartened by it, warmed by it, enlivened by it.

It was now time to turn the season, to leave winter and step into spring. Everyone picked up the boughs lying about the temple, these vestiges of winter that were cut on winter solstice, when we had gathered to celebrate the sun's return. We put the boughs on the fire as a welcoming beacon to greet the light.

And what a beacon it was.

Amid our glee at burning winter, leaving it behind, the dry boughs sparked and crackled on the fire. At first, lots of boughs went into the pit at once and it looked as though the fire might have been doused, buried under the greenery of winter. Smoke gushed upward in a column, straight out the roof of the temple. I was awed.

And then, flames. At first the flames barely peeked out of the column of smoke, scarcely discernable. Moments later they engulfed everything and became a pillar of fire, reaching to the roof of the temple. Peals of laughter and joy rang out, and we all stepped judiciously back. The dark and chill of the night vanished and the brilliant light of the fire energized us to the core. We kept on until all the greenery of winter had been given to the fire and we felt the light of spring buzzing in our bones.

As the flames abated, we began the sweeping. Accompanied by the chanting of all those in the temple, the priestesses took up their brooms and swept the floor. Moving sunwise (clockwise) around the temple, following the path of the sun, we swept the remainder of winter into the fire pit. I remembered the crisp cold day I gathered the boughs for the Winter Solstice ceremony and the intimate morning I spent in the temple the next day, sitting among the fragrant greenery. I contemplated the joys of the long winter nights in front of the fire, hot chocolate with cinnamon steaming in the cup, warming my nose. This was the turn of the season, and the hours of languid, dreamy winter sleep would give way to the growth of spring. I swept with bittersweet excitement, joined with my sister priestesses in the sacred spring cleaning, readying us all for the growth spurt of spring.

Rituals: The First Day of Summer

The maypole is a festive Euro-Pagan tradition to celebrate May Day, but a philosophical minefield for Goddess Spirituality folk and feminists. Readers not familiar with the internecine politics between duo-theistic "Lord and Lady" Pagans and Goddess Spirituality folk might see this as a nonissue. And those who are familiar with this are probably already thinking about skipping this section, firm in their belief that the other side hasn't seen the light of truth.

The maypole dance is certainly an old tradition, and according to Nathaniel Hawthorne's short story, "The Maypole of Merry Mount," it was practiced in early New England. But for me the most important aspect of the maypole dance is that it is a lot of fun, and fairly simple. Tie long strips of cloth or ribbon to the top of a pole, and set the pole upright in the ground. A crown of flowers can be placed at the top of the pole too. Have everyone gather in circle around the pole and grab a ribbon. Sometimes people circle in a female/male/female/male pattern, and sometimes they just crowd around; either way is good. To prepare for the dance, every other person faces the opposite direction, so that half of the circle will move sunwise, or *deosil* (clockwise), and the other

half will move widdershins (counterclockwise). The music starts,
ribbons are in hand. The people facing sunwise start with their
ribbons high in the air, the widdershins with their ribbons below,
and they pass each other, either stepping over or going under the
ribbon. Facing the next person, each moves her or his ribbon in
the opposite way, up or down, and they pass again, going under
or stepping over. This continues until the maypole ribbons are
wrapped around the pole in a beautiful crisscross fashion. It is a
delightful dance. Everyone sees everyone else face to face, duck-
ing and weaving over others' ribbons. It is really fun.

But I had some misgivings about the maypole, mostly with
its modern connotations. If the pole is interpreted as simply a
phallus and the ritual revolves around phallus worship with the
supreme act as female/male human fertility, then that is really
not in line with my own path of Goddess Spirituality seeking
to honor the Divine Female. In my worldview, the Divine Male
is already widely honored and is not in need of extra adulation.
I wanted to refashion this ceremony with an emphasis on the
Divine Female and her central place in creation.

I began investigating the source of the maypole to find out
its roots. At the same time my academic self was delving into
the dusty annals of rites and lore, magick occurred in the desert.
As I was wondering what kind of pole to use, how it might work
logistically as well as philosophically, and then almost discard-
ing the whole idea because I could not resign myself to going
to Home Depot and buying a piece of lumber for this sacred
rite—just at this moment, all of my intellectual wonderings were
brought down by a magickal event.

Ben found a ship's mast in the desert.

The mast was twenty-five feet long, of weathered wood, and
still had the rigging attached. It was near the turtle-shaped fire
pit where Corbin Harney led his sunrise ceremonies. I took this

mast as a portent to move forward, both on the research and the logistical planes.

In terms of research, I began with one of the oldest symbols of the tree trunk, which is the Mesopotamian goddess Asherah. She is symbolized by a pillar and is frequently mentioned in the Old Testament of the Bible. One of the things that intrigued me about the pillar/tree trunk iconography of Asherah was that in this guise she did not have a face or a woman's body. In my view, she is Goddess of the Earth, and she inhabits what could be considered a humanish form—the tree.[20]

I considered the symbolic use of trees in different spiritual traditions, such as the Tree of Life, the Kabbalah, the Nordic *Yggdrasil*. Coupled with that was my personal use of a tree in my shamanic journeys to climb to the upper world or descend to the lower world. I reflected on the tree as a symbol for understanding the idea of gift. The tree gives freely of itself, and the fruit contains the seeds of its progeny, its continued existence. The fruit is eaten and the seeds are returned to the earth, grow, and are fertilized. As well, the tree provides a habitat for animals of the air and Earth—birds and cats and snakes. The tree is the connection between the Earth and the sky.

I began being the tree. At night, I stood on the ground, feeling my feet stretch downward, my toes lengthen, each turning into a root searching for rich soil and water. I felt the trunk of my body solidify, strong and upright. I put my arms above my head and stretched my limbs long, then my fingers longer, branching out to the starry night, touching the stars.

I was the divine connection between sky and Earth; my roots drank from waters deep. I listened to the whispering of the stars.

And I began to understand fertility—fertility in a meta-sense. I remembered my oft-given speech on fertility in response to those who marginalize female deities with the term "fertility goddess." I would counter that fertility is the stuff of life—all life. Without fertility, there are no plants, no animals, no humans, no food, no sustenance, and ultimately, no life. The sacred joining, the coming together, and the spark of life that is produced—these are fertility. To reduce the concept of fertility to solely human reproduction is egocentric at best. To reduce a goddess to solely the idea of human fertility is specious. Fertility means the continuation of life, which we all should have not just a vested interest in, but also take great joy in celebrating.

Our May Tree became a community project. I imagined a snake on the pole, winding from the Earth to the sky, symbolizing the energy that is transmitted in this divine connection. From the beginning, one of our temple regulars, an Army veteran and Jeep enthusiast named Justin, wanted to restore this weathered wood mast to its original majesty. On the weekends Justin and his wife Angie would come to the temple, and he patiently sanded until the wood was smooth while Angie and I worked on our tans.

The second part was designing the snake. Fortunately, I had a snake on hand. I had received a beautiful priestess-trained Red-tailed boa constrictor from my fellow priestess Sylvia Brallier. As she said, a temple priestess needs a snake. Sylvia trained this beautiful and friendly snake and named her Asherah.[21] Then Jen, both priestess and artist, had the marvelous idea of letting Asherah crawl up the pole and trace her pattern as she slithered from the bottom to the top. It seemed the perfect destiny—Asherah climbing the Asherah.

One sunny afternoon, we watched Asherah soak up the leaf-filtered sun under the cottonwood tree as she climbed the mast from bottom to top. The pattern of her movements was surprising to me. She did not ascend in a barber's-pole fashion, as we imagined she would. She wound in different ways, her coils lying in odd and seemingly uncomfortable patterns. But who was I to decide what was uncomfortable for a snake? Jen drew as Asherah ascended, tracking the pattern of her climb.

Then Justin produced his favorite woodworking tool—a dremel. He spent more weekends carving the body of the snake into the smooth wood, following the serpentine lines Jen had drawn, sometimes losing the thread but always finding it again. After the body outlines were carved, Jen returned to fill in the patterns on the body, and Asherah's markings became yet another symbol. The markings of the Red-tailed boa are saddle-shaped ovals spaced by a circle in between. The circles change from light dun-colored to almost black along her six-foot span. Through her carefully honed artist's eye, Jen interpreted these as the moon phases. Thus, the twenty-five-foot Asherah on the mast was decorated with the thirteen yearly moon phases, from new to full and new again. The end of the pole became her head, and Jen exquisitely captured Asherah's enigmatic and slightly bemused look.

On another weekend, Justin carved the moon shapes. Daily the pole became an increasingly beautiful work of sacred art. The final steps were painting and staining. Jen and Lily tag-teamed the painting, along with others from our artist community, and Justin returned with new hardware for the rigging, shined and polished. I was in charge of marine varnish, the final step.

After a year of communal effort, the mast from the desert became a work of sacred art. We ceremoniously planted the May Tree upright in the ground, the ribbons from the previous year buried beneath it along with offerings. Asherah's face turned to the sky, looking ever upward, her tail buried deep within the earth. As Jen said, Asherah, my snake, had become our Asherah, our pillar, our symbol of life, growth, and the divine connection that is the essence of life.

We danced around Asherah that first year. We wrote our prayers on our ribbons and bound them tightly as we sang and danced, our circle coiling earth to sky. We danced to weave our prayers and dreams, to be the tree, the divine connection. We danced to celebrate the life force, the fertility, the love of the land around us. We danced to awaken the fertility within ourselves, to become one with the season, to set flower that would bear fruit and continue the cycle of nourishment and sustenance, giving our unique gifts of life.

The Priestesses Gather Magick Brooms

Though it is always tempting to relegate brooms to the favorite mode of transportation of the caricature Hallowe'en witch or, in a modern context, the sexier Harry Potter sport models, it is more instructive to look at brooms in their domestic function. We hang brooms above or stand them next to our doors to cleanse and sweep all that enters our homes. Each year at Samhain we burn our brooms, officially leaving the old year and bringing in the new.

The September Full Moon ritual was dedicated to broom making. The morning of the ritual, Jen and I drove up to the trailhead of Mount Charleston to gather sticks for broom handles and grasses and herbs for the brooms.

At an elevation of 11,916 feet, Mt. Charleston is the highest peak of the Spring Mountains, just twenty minutes east of the temple. This wilderness area is a green jewel in the desert. For me, Mt. Charleston was a reminder of Oregon, and for Jen it was a connection to Mammoth, California. Jen's round faerie-like face was framed by her nut-brown hair. She is a veritable kitchen witch; my favorite of her brews is her iced tea with the sweet herb melissa. That morning as we got out of the car, stepping into this completely different ecosystem that had both of us remembering other places we had called home, we surrendered ourselves to the plants around us, asking for their bounty.

A cool breeze lightly touched us as it carried the crisp, fresh news of the imminent arrival of winter. The breeze was the microphone, making audible the whisperings of the trees. The conifers whistled, and the aspens rattled in response. We had come upon the plants in mid-preparation for winter. Seeds were scattering, pine cones falling and digging in, the heads of rabbit-tail grass turning from yellow to lighter-than-air puffs of seed-laden clouds, hoping to catch a ride on the wind. Stalks bent in beautiful arches, heads reaching to the ground, moving their seeds closer to home. Only vestiges of the royal purple of thistle remained, as the grey pallor of winter cloaked her and her flowers followed suit, turning to wind-friendly puffs ready to fly to new homes and burrow in the earth.

Most of the lamb's ears had flowered, but some were late, pushing a few blooms out, knowing full well the freezing consequences of their tardiness. Maybe the stalks had spent too much time reveling in the warmth of the sun, not wanting to push their energy out yet in flowers, or perhaps a seed had been slow in germinating and was desperately trying to live a full life in only half a lifetime. A few of the lamb's ears seemed to have resigned themselves to the fate of dying on this Earth without progeny; stalwart, they looked far off and found the eye of winter, held its gaze and, firmly rooted, stared back, intending to live this moment to its fullest despite the consequences.

There were other lamb's ears that had spread seeds, carrying on their sacred duty. However, one late bloomer was going to live at her own pace, not accepting the idea that the beautiful yellow flowers peeking out were doomed or useless. She ignored the tide of warnings, the general murmurings from the surrounding lamb's ears that had already bloomed and let go of their seed. She stood tall and proud, her yellow flowers displayed on the

eve of the Harvest Moon, filling my heart with love and courage. I left an offering of my hair—my bloom—in honor of her
perseverance.

We had our bags and shears ready. We looked around, feeling the magick of the moments when autumn wanes and winter
creeps closer with silent footsteps. We turned from each other to
walk in separate directions, to find the plants willing to be cut,
wanting to serve, interested in living in a new place, above a
doorway, with someone who would appreciate their gifts.

I turned to cut and remembered, in the face of the purity
and love of the plants, that Jen and I had not begun the smudging ritual. I called to her, and we met in the trail. I lit the sage
smudge mix, our priestess blend, and the smoke brought back
the life of every plant, every intention. The smoke lifted out of
me the weight of the past days.

Jen and I smudged each other, recounting our prayers: That
our ears will hear the plants that come willingly. That the plants
will come and purify the homes, and that we will live in a place
of peaceful security, where we can live our highest good. That
the seeds still on the plants will become our seeds, will hold our
dreams that will burrow in our souls and gestate over the long
winter. That the plants will bring us their wisdom, and that we
will have our hearts open to receive. Jen and I were enveloped by
the dream, smoke swirling and prayers forming.

We turned and walked through the forest, awakened to
the energies around us and charged with purpose. Jen slipped
into her faerie self, walking among the chatter of the plants and
herbs, listening as she always does. I set out, clippers in hand,
opening my ears and heart to the plants' musings.

Sacred Land, Sacred Sky

During my first days as priestess, I spent an afternoon in the temple chatting with a visitor. I shared some of my personal fears and doubts regarding my ability to lead. I cannot remember her name or her connection to the temple, but I remember what she said to me. I can clearly envision us standing in the dusty parking lot as she prepared to leave. Her hand grasped my forearm, lending physical emphasis to her words. She looked me directly in the eye and spoke: "The land will support you." I did not know what she meant, but as time went on, it became clear. The land was an ally, ready to help me become my best, to help me to connect, to be a friend. I had never known land as a friend before. Certain trees, for sure. But never land.

When I began praying and making offerings on this land, I was shocked. It was so easy to pray here. The land shimmered with the breath of the Divine. I opened myself and the land opened herself, wide. The water answered my call. The goddesses in the temple emanated life. Sekhmet smiled. Faeries danced.

The land was sacred to me. It contained my blood, my tears, my hair, my footprints. Since there was a septic system, the land held everything that I had eaten, everything I had washed away. I felt I was truly of the land, and the land was of me.

At the beginning of each ceremony, we honored the four directions and an element associated with each: east and air;

south and fire; west and water; north and earth. Many times
when the directions are called, they are written with a wet, lush
environment in mind: cool breeze, deep black earth, rushing
rivers, dense forests. But these images did not reflect the desert
land, a dry, thriving environment. I wrote a call of directions
specifically for this land, for this place, for this temple:

> Winds of the mind, open free.
> Breath of life, breathe in me.
> Red flame of truth, burning pure.
> Spark of life, ignite me.
> Water of my soul, blood of earth.
> Spring of life, wash me.
> Bones of rock, sand, and earth.
> Roots of life, ground me.

Sacred Land in America: The Great Disconnect

The idea of sacred land in our modern times seems incongru-
ous. What could possibly be sacred about our modern world, our
modern life? It is that idea that I tried to counter at the temple
with every ritual, every prayer.

I feel the need to live in sacred communion with the land
that provides me with water, that feeds me, houses me, and
clothes me. Ultimately it is the *land*, not the water company, the
construction company, or the grocery store that supports my
existence. I might pay these different entities for their services,
but ultimately the source that I should honor for sustaining my
life is the land.

Sacred land is a place where spirit and matter meet, where
beings go to encounter the Divine. It is a place where these
meetings have taken place, over and over. It is the place we go

when we cannot find the Divine within ourselves or in our own backyards. It is the place where the Divine awaits us. I did not know the power of this, the reality of this, until I began to pray on this land.

I began to understand why people fight and die to protect sacred land. I understood why people risk their lives to endure storms, floods, and fires to stay on the land. For the first time, I truly, viscerally knew the power, beauty, and the irreplaceable nature of sacred land.

My new feelings offered me a glimpse of the depth of grief and sorrow for the loss of sacred land that Native Americans have endured. I knew that if the federal government were to come to me and offer to trade the temple for similar acreage somewhere else, I would refuse. And if they told me I had no choice, I would fight. Because this land, this temple land, held the accumulated energy of over almost two decades of daily prayers and offerings. This land held the ancient prayers and gratitude of all of those who lived here, drank from this spring, danced on this earth. That was irreplaceable.

I wept that I came to this knowing so late. I grieved for all that my people, my fellow Euro-American conquerors, have misunderstood, for all the irreparable harm we have caused, for all that we have destroyed. I grieved for the state of spiritual poverty that I lived in, disconnected from this land.

As I contemplated the idea of sacred land in modern America and how to bring others in communion with the land, one thing became glaringly apparent. Many Euro-Americans feel that the land called the United States of America has sacred significance to Native Americans but not to them. This was certainly a point to ponder.

While the term *sacred land* may indeed refer to land within the boundaries of the modern United States, the term *Holy Land* singularly refers to Palestine and Israel. While considering this, I began to see the disconnect between the current dominant Euro-American culture and the land that feeds it.

The basis for this disconnect might be seen as an outgrowth of the predominant Abrahamic spiritual heritage of the people in the United States. The majority of Americans claim Christianity, Judaism, and Islam as their religion.[22] For them, the Holy Land is indeed Israel and Palestine, not North America.

Then there is the consideration of the philosophical heritage of Euro-Americans. This heritage gives us the rationalist world view, the view that there is a demarcation between the sacred and the profane, between human and the land, between human and animal, between human and plant. This demarcation of difference serves to desacralize almost everything except possibly the loftiest humans, the loftiest places, the loftiest actions. This desacralization allows humans to view nature as a soulless entity whose sole purpose is to physically support the human race, which in turn allows humans to use nature for any purpose they see fit, placing humans outside the context of nature.

Thus, the present state of Euro-Americans' spiritual connection to the land is horribly distorted. On one hand, the Holy Land lies somewhere else. On the other hand, Euro-Americans don't have a spiritual connection to the land; they simply use the land or at best "steward" the land.

This situation seems very bleak and without ready answers.

The Personal Politics of Place: White Euro-American Priestess, Black African Goddess, Native American Newe Land

Most of the time when I was in the desert, the past, present, and future of human politics and actions in regard to the land were not foremost. I tried to listen and learn from the spirits, the animals, the plants, the land, and to understand or at least discern the Divine Mysteries embodied by Sekhmet. But, truly, I was smack-dab in the middle of the political fray, whether I liked it or not.

I am a white woman, a Euro-American of uninvestigated ancestry, firmly upper middle class and educated. I was a priestess to an Egyptian goddess, a black goddess from Egypt, northern Africa. I was paid by a wealthy white Euro-American philanthropist, an oil heiress, a fellow Texan, who built the temple as a promise kept for a prayer answered by a black African goddess.

I lived on land an heiress had purchased and then ceded back to the Western Shoshone, who had claimed this as their land in the Ruby Valley Treaty in the 1800s, and who were my landlords. I was a white feminist leading goddess-centered rituals on recognized Native American sacred land to predominately Euro-Americans. I often felt like an amoeba in a Petri dish, placed there by a mad but curious scientist-academic who wanted to do an experiment on post-colonial issues.

This situation served as a metaphysical backhoe, digging up every feeling of white guilt and self-doubt fermenting in the compost of my soul. Exposed to light, this was smelly, unsightly, repugnant, and nauseating. But it was necessary for me to get my hands dirty, to look, touch, and recognize every bit of putrefying personal refuse. By turning my compost, the heat of the decomposition process spread more evenly. I hope that internal transformation is still taking place and my internal soil is nourishing my outward blooms.

Fueled by self-doubt and guilt, I began the process of cataloguing my inner workings. Was I secretly harboring thoughts that would be considered racist? Was it true that because I was white that I was racist, no matter what? And that any other thought, any thought that I was not racist, was illusion that I spun

for myself to make myself feel better while I feasted and pros-
pered on the backs of people of color? Was I an evil person? If
not evil, was I a silly do-gooder? Did people of color laugh at me,
seeing through my persona, my illusion that by doing something
I thought was helping, I was actually just relieving my white
guilt? And were those acts of goodwill hollow? Stupid? Foolish?
And was I living this life in denial of my white privilege?

And did this denial spread to my spiritual life? Was I a New
Age plastic shaman, excoriated and ridiculed by real shamans?
Were my actions hollow? Was my ego lying to me, showing me
as a powerful spiritual woman, when in actuality I was a fraud?
Was I kidding myself that I had any connection to the Divine?
As a white woman, could I ever be a true priestess to an African
goddess? Was my ego tricking me? Playing with me? Was my
whole spiritual life just simply feeding my ego, my white ego,
with no true basis?

Was I lacking in capability? Was I capable of being deeply
connected to the Earth, being a priestess, even though I was
white? Because to be white seemed to make me silly and super-
cilious, make me deluded, shrouded in a white dreamy illusion.
How could I know what real life was about? It seemed to me
I had ignored those who tried to tell me the truth, that I was
stupid, unable to grasp the really big truths that were out there. I
was unable to be filled with the Divine because there was really
nothing to fill. I was porous, unconnected, like a balloon with
a hole in it. Useless. A superfluous ornament. Just something
to "bring a little class" to the place. A "fluffy bunny," unable to
grasp the deep dark mysteries. Afraid to get my hands dirty in
"real" spiritual and political work.

I heard the echoes of the words of Felipe, a Paiute peace
activist I met at a Nevada Test Site demonstration, whirl around
and around my head: First they took our land, and now they

are taking our religion. I was "they." And every time I used a feather, burned sage, and danced and sang the sounds from my heart, I wondered if I was following the spiritual guidance of the land or stealing the culture of a people that my ancestors had grievously wronged.

I wanted to hear my self-doubt. I wanted to hear these pieces, to know that these realities could exist. But I wanted to hear them and not let them break me at the knees, not let them crumble me. Hear them, but not let them cut so deep into my heart that I was immobilized, unable to even think. It was stultifying to be plagued with self-doubt.

Sylvia once passed on to me a saying that she had learned from a Native American shaman: An arrow only goes in where there is already a hole. And I wanted that hole to be mended.

I wanted to be whole. I wanted to hear, really hear, the words, stories, anger, and fears of others. I wanted to see their arrows, be able to look at them, examine them, feel them in my hands. I wanted to feel them hit my skin, but not pierce my skin, not pierce it and drain out all of my essential fluids, leaving me a tattered mess, haunted by voices in my dreams and giving form to my self-doubt, night after night. I didn't want to wake up in the morning hearing the voices that told me that I was silly, superfluous, and living indolently and unconsciously in a white privileged illusion. That was not where I was. That was not who I was.

I wanted to be firm in my own understanding of myself, firm but not imperious. Firm but open. I wanted to know that I was a person of worth, that I was able to know and feel deeply. That I had a true, honest, beautiful, and real relationship with the Divine. That I certainly had pieces of life that I lived in illusion, but that I struggled to move out of that illusion. That I recognized and struggled with my egocentrism.

I wanted to be able to be a spiritual leader for this temple. I

wanted to be able to bring people to the threshold of the Divine
and to bring the Divine to the threshold, and to make the opportunity available for the two to meet in sacred communion. And I
could not do that if I was drowning in self-doubt, if I felt that my
color and my heritage made me less worthy. I needed to believe
in myself and hold myself in absolute love, compassion, and
honesty.

And in the end, it was the land that I went back to, time and
again, for strength.

Water from Above and Below: The Rain and the Spring

Sacred land is often associated with springs, waterfalls, streams,
and rivers, because water is one of the sources of life. The Temple Spring manifests this visually. In a sparsely vegetated area,
the spring gives life to the towering cottonwoods, the abundant
creosote, the thorny mesquite, as well as providing sustenance
for all the birds and wildlife in the area. If one wants to see the
life-giving properties of water, the Temple Spring is one of the
best examples I can imagine.

I did not truly appreciate rain until I lived in the desert. During the decade I lived on the Oregon Coast in Tillamook County,
I reached a certain level of appreciation and understanding of
the gifts of rain. Water was a part of my daily life, and it was not
unusual to have over one hundred inches of rain each year.

The roads were flooded innumerable times; we went without
power for days after heavy storms and floods. I planned my life
around the water, the rivers, and the tides so that I could make it
home before high tide pushed the water in the rivers up and over
their banks onto the roads. Water determined when I would go
to the store and stock up and when I couldn't leave the house for
fear of not being able to get back. I learned about water, came to

respect its power, but I don't know that I appreciated it. I took it for granted that it would rain.

Then I moved to the temple, to the land that averages less than five inches of rain per year. Friends of mine who had moved to Las Vegas from upper New York state told me that they were in their house for three years before it rained. Rain isn't a given in southern Nevada.

However, during my first months at the temple, that first winter, it rained almost incessantly. I kept thinking—hey, I moved to the desert! I want sun! But it kept raining. Puddles formed. The earth was soaked.

People said that the new priestess had brought in the life-giving rain, the rain from the Pacific Northwest. I felt like the agent of change, the one to bring water to the parched and thirsty land. Maybe I had a special gift, linked to bringing water. As I privately complained about all the rain, I publicly smiled at the references to myself as a rain-bringer.

And it kept raining all winter. While the average rainfall is 4.5 inches per year, in that winter of 2004–2005 Las Vegas received 8.33 inches of rain, and I'm sure we got more rain out in Cactus Springs. While it was raining at our house, it was snowing at nearby Mt. Charleston, our local ski resort. Ben and I enjoyed a spectacular snowboarding season during this peak snow year. I waited impatiently for the days of unrelenting desert sun to begin. But it just kept raining.

Then came the spring. Grasses grew all around our house. Small purple flowers bloomed in a thick carpet around the temple. In Death Valley, flowers that had not bloomed for decades stuck their heads out through the desert floor and blossomed. Spring was dazzling. I luxuriated in the beauty born from the rain, and when people remarked that I had brought the rain and the beautiful spring, when those at the temple took pride that their priestess had brought the rain from the Pacific Northwest, well, I just smiled. I didn't overtly take credit, but I didn't dissuade them either. I smiled, feeling that somehow I had helped bring the rain.

That was our first spring in the desert.

During the next two years of my stay as priestess, the rainfall dropped precipitously. In 2006, the rainfall was a mere 1.69 inches for the entire year. The spring of 2007, hardly any tiny purple flowers bloomed because of the lack of rain. There were no grasses growing around our house, except for the patch underneath the cottonwoods, fed by underground water. The wildflowers were sparse. The rabbit population had boomed during the rainy year, so now there wasn't enough for them to eat. We found their dried, desiccated bodies in the desert. The coyotes looked painfully thin. The new growth on the Joshua trees and yuccas was barely visible.

During our last spring, the rain was almost imperceptible. The fuchsia -colored blooms on the beavertail cactus were one of the few heralds of the changing of the season. There was just less of everything. It was quite obvious what the rain brought. Even with the generous underground water around the temple, which kept the cottonwoods and mesquite trees alive and green, it was the rain that brought life to the desert floor. Without rain, there were no tiny purple flowers. Without rain, there was no abundance. Without rain, the dry was unrelenting. Without rain, there was simply less.

I was keenly aware of my hubris. And I set my mind and heart to always welcome the rain.

I have grown to consciously welcome the rain at every opportunity and to change whatever keeps me from wholeheartedly welcoming it. If it rains when it is inconvenient, say, during a ritual, I move myself to a mental space of being able to openly and freely love the rain and not think of it as a pest. Rain is precious. I welcome it, love it, no matter when it comes. Is there something outside that could get wet? I bring it in and welcome the rain. Is it raining hard during the annual Renaissance Faire when I'm débuting my new custom leather corset? I stand in the rain and get wet and reach deep inside to love the rain.

Living in the desert, I wanted to open myself completely to the rain, to its possibility. I wanted to live in a state of genuine gratitude about the rain.

The Temple Spring and Lessons for the Priestess

Officially, the name of the spring by the temple is Cactus Spring; however, we call it the Temple Spring or Patricia's Spring. Patricia loved the spring, and she and her husband Al cared for it and cleaned the area around it. The spring is a popular stop for travelers for a picnic or a rest, and while many are respectful of the area, some thoughtlessly dump trash. Patricia put bins in the parking lot so people would have a place to put their trash. When she went to the spring one day and found that someone had dumped a car battery into it, that was it. She dedicated herself to persuading the Bureau of Land Management (BLM), which has jurisdiction of the land surrounding the temple, to build a fence around the spring to protect it. Eventually the fence was built and the land around it slowly restored with native plantings. It is truly an oasis.

The spring is surrounded by cottonwood trees and the path leading to it is shaded by a towering cottonwood, its long branches reaching wide. Curving to the right, the path opens to a clearing with a grassy knoll encircled by three young cottonwoods and one older, dying one. I call the young trees the Three Sisters and the older one the Crone. The Crone's bare upper branches are in stark contrast to the numerous leaves of the Three Sisters.

The bank encircling the spring has a dry and grassy crescent on the south side, perfect for communing with the water and all who are drawn to it. This spring teems with life, including fish, turtles, frogs, grasses, and birds. The banks show the signs of the various animals that depend on it, with hoof and paw prints in the mud and tall grass blades bent from trampling.

Since my arrival at the temple, I had spent time and energy feeding the temple and Sekhmet; I had not really thought of much else. I was Priestess of the Temple, and I wanted to make sure everything there was well cared for, that the temple was welcoming and full of energy. I did begin singing to the mountains to the south, the Spring Mountains, mostly to bring their energy inside. But essentially I restricted my focus to the temple and the area directly around it. I suppose that is one of the drawbacks to being myopically task-oriented, which I admittedly am.

An Eastern Shoshone peace activist came to the temple one bright summer day during a protest at the Nevada Test Site. He walked the land and then came into the temple. We chatted and walked around the temple and then up the path to the spring. When we got there, he turned to look at me and said, "The spring says that you are not singing to it. Why hasn't anyone been singing to this spring? It needs to be sung to."

It was true—I hadn't been singing to the spring. I sang to the temple, to the goddesses, to the mountains, to the plants, to the rain—but I hadn't been singing to the spring.

I was taken aback. And he made no mention of the good work that I had done with the temple land. Maybe all of my singing had been for naught. Maybe I was just a fraud, or simply stupid and incompetent. I had obviously missed the most important piece, the spring. I felt deflated and angry. My ego was bruised. I felt like reciting a litany of what I *had* done.

But he was right; I needed to sing to the spring and bring

it into the rituals. So I began to chant to the spring, adding it to my rounds of chanting. I began holding rituals at the spring and using the water in ceremonies. I began calling the elements into our rituals, specifically calling the water of the Temple Spring. And I thank the peace activist for being the messenger for water.

I learned to sing to water by watching Corbin Harney, the spiritual leader of the Newe (the Western Shoshone), the indigenous people of the land. At every gathering he would sing to water, encouraging us to do the same:

> *Naraborochi*, that's in my words [the Newe language], that's water. Water is something that really, we have to appreciate. Those are the reasons why we have to sing about those things, 'cause if it wasn't for water, there would be no life on this Earth. We have to sing to 'em, sing to the life of the water, the spirit of the water and so forth. So the water can be happier, the water can continue to flow. We have to make that water spirit at least as happy as can be.[23]

Corbin always said that everyone should pray in whatever way they felt comfortable, that all prayers were valid. But that we needed to pray and sing together, to sing to the water, the air, and the earth. When I heard Corbin pray in the Newe language on the ancestral Newe land, it was as if the very earth rose to dance with his song. It was as if an old friend, a lovingly familiar voice, called to it. It was beautiful.

So I sing to the spring. Singing to the spring binds me to it, brings us together, and especially brings me closer. In this world, it is easy to live very separated from what sustains and nurtures us. But by singing and chanting and being closer together, we become one. Actually, we are one; it's just that I have somehow mentally extricated myself from being fully cognizant and aware of my relationship with water. I sing and chant to give my gift of song to the water, and this has the effect of putting me in the web of life, in this glorious oneness of all. Maybe someday water will recognize my voice and dance with me. But I think I have years of singing to go before that happens. For now, I will keep singing, remembering Corbin and the other messengers of water.

I believe in a reciprocal universe, and that we as humans are part of it all. We are no more privileged than anything else—not water, earth, plants, animals. And I have a responsibility not to privilege myself. Knowing water as an entity and recognizing water as a fellow being, a live being, moves me into partnership with water, in a reciprocal relationship with water.

This is, of course, nothing new. For millennia, people have been living this way in countless cultures around the world. These beliefs are the basis of spiritual traditions, including many Native American traditions. And many Native Americans have held on to these beliefs through the colonization of their ancestral lands and the decimation of their culture. And for this preservation, this perseverance, I am grateful.

I was raised in a culture that saw nature as inanimate, something to be used, though it made me aware of my responsibility to use it wisely. I now try and live in partnership, seeing myself as part of nature. It is at once a simple and complex change of perspective. It shifts my sense of responsibility from myself as an individual to the collective, to all.

Invocations and Ritual to Water[24]

I wove both the element of water and the Temple Spring into our rituals, to both honor and extol their properties as well as to bring people's awareness to the waters without and within, to their own connection to water.

Water is the source of life. We come from water, and eventually we return to water. All life comes from the ocean, and all of us are born from the oceans inside our mothers' wombs.

Water follows the line of least resistance but is itself irresistible. Water has no clear or fixed boundaries. Water nourishes everything it touches. Water rolls over obstacles but wears away the hardest granite. Water is the power of small relentless acts against seemingly vast obstacles. Water changes its shape, fits into any vessel, without losing its essence. In this way, water reminds me that I can be flexible without losing myself. Waters are ever changing and ever unfinished, as we are.

All water constantly circulates between the oceans, continents, and atmosphere; all water is connected. When we sing and honor water in one place, we are connected to all the water all over the planet. And if the theory is true that water on Earth originates from a frozen comet, then water also connects us with the vast cosmos.

When I decided to sing to the Temple Spring, to sing to water, I realized that I didn't have a song. Corbin sang in Newe, which was beautiful, but it wasn't my language. Songs about the ocean water seemed not quite right for a spring in the desert. Songs about rain didn't work well for me either. I needed a song for this spring on this land, the Temple Spring. And I needed a song in my own language, to follow my own tradition. So I wrote my own.

To honor the element of water, I wrote a chant that we often used at the beginning of ritual in the temple:

Waters of my soul
Blood of the earth
Spring of life
Wash over me

Singing, chanting, invoking, and honoring water awakens my water within and connects me to the waters of the Earth.

The Wind

The wind is literally a force of nature in the desert. I realized after being there for a couple of months that I would need to surrender to it, to learn to live with it, just as I had learned to live with the rain on the Oregon coast.

The area around the temple is flat, with mountains off in the distance on the south and north sides. The wind usually came barreling from west to east, like a herd of wild animals, like a tidal wave. There was nothing ethereal or ephemeral about this wind. It was solid. I had always associated wind with rain and storms, but in the desert the wind was just the wind. Blowing with amazing force, as if it gathered strength over the desert, the wind hit our little house like a wave, as if we were the only thing it had to buffet against.

I remember the night of our first big wind storm. The wind howled, banging against the thin trailer walls. I was sure that the whole thing would just tip over, and it was hard not to flashback to scenes from Dorothy and *The Wizard of Oz*. When Ben and I slept on the porch during wind storms, we would hear the plastic lawn furniture crashing about, the tinkle of glass somewhere breaking, and wonder if we had left clothes on the line. We pulled lots of shirts out of the bramble.

One night we slept on the Starbed in thirty- to forty-mile-per-hour winds, just to prove we could. I tucked in the covers facing the wind, but the top blanket still managed to get blown off. Ben scrambled down to pull our blanket out of the creosote bushes, Russian tumbleweeds hanging from it.

In the temple the wind would wreak havoc, pillows thrown everywhere, offerings tipped over and often broken. One day I was walking in the gully quite a distance from the temple and found a pillow there, blown far from its place next to the statue of Sekhmet.

In summer, the wind was like a hairdryer, blowing dry hot air sometimes speckled with sand. Facing that force, I could feel every bit of my body's moisture sucked into the wind, like a paper towel soaking up a spill. I never used moisturizer living in Oregon, but I went through bottles and bottles in the Nevada desert.

But the gentle winds, they filled my heart. In autumn and winter when the leaves on the cottonwoods were dry, the wind blew gently through. It sounded like rain, or sleet at times. It was one of the most soothing sounds, like a little stream running overhead, the gentle water tripping over polished stones. The wind was a great comfort to my water-loving Oregon self.

When I first came out to the temple, I talked to Patricia about the wind. She said that she loved the wind because it wiped everything clean. And so I began to think of the winds like that, winds that would smudge the land, winds that would smudge me.

I began to see the wind as an ally, a faithful and strong friend. A gentle friend reminding me of the sound of water over smooth stones. An amusing friend that would rearrange the pillows and secret some of them away for me to find in unusual places, provoking a laugh at the incongruity of it all.

Dancing with the Elements: Air and Ritual

The structure of the temple forces those inside to interact with the elements. The structure opens to the heat and cold, the roof opens to the rain, and the doors open to the wind. The wind, whether present or absent, is an element in every ritual. No wind, and the smoke drifts up through the roof. Wind from the west, and those standing in the east get smoke in their faces—doubly smudged. High winds, and the fire is difficult to light. No wind, and the fire is difficult to light. Too breezy, and the candles go out. As priest-ess, I found that I had to surrender frequently to the wind.

One full moon night we did a ceremony in high winds. The winds were a steady twenty to thirty miles per hour with highs around forty mph. It was crazy. I couldn't keep any of the can-dles lit in the temple, even the ones at the bottom of long glass jars. I wasn't sure I could light the fire, and then I wasn't sure what it would do if I did get it lit.

There was no way I could get a sage wand or charcoal lit in the wind, so I had everyone gather, open their arms, and be smudged and cleansed with the wind. I turned full face into it, and let go. I let go of the day, let go of harbored feelings, let go of worries about the ceremony, let go of all those things that didn't serve me well. And the wind took them away. Far away. I felt cleansed through and through.

It had been raining recently, and the grounds around the temple were relatively wet. Since there were only ten or so of us in the temple, I decided to take a chance and light the fire. And oh, did it light. The fire was wild that night. Leaping, jumping, swirling, casting fantastic shadows on the temple walls. We stood in awe of the fire, moving to stay out of the flames' reach. The playful, joyful, bounding fire was infectious; I remember being stunned into laughter and delight.

I began to think of the wind as a messenger as well. We started knotting prayer ties on the creosote bushes surrounding the temple. Those prayer ties waved vigorously and fervently. At the end of our ceremonies, as we prayed for peace, I imagined our prayers carried on the wind, whispering into the ears of all those who the winds passed: May all know peace.

Stars

The sparseness of the desert lends itself to the sky view. After the heat of the day, the cool nights call, and the stars begin their nightly procession. It is enchanting to have the sky view from east to west, north to south. Sometimes I think I can see the curve of the Earth. Ben and I became such avid night-sky watchers that we put our Netflix account on hold. We preferred to sit outside at night to watch the sky's feature presentation.

We would go out to the Starbed at twilight and watch the stars come out, seeing the brightest ones—Sirius, Capella, the North Star—and planets like Venus and Mars. Then the constellations would come into focus—the Big Dipper, Cassiopeia—and finally the background of stars would fill in. My challenge was to try to keep the constellations in focus among the millions of glints of light.

Seeing the stars night after night awakened a new consciousness in me. I would see them move from one side of the sky to the other, see how they moved every night and every season, tracing their seemingly oddly oblique path. The sky was no longer a static painting; it was a dynamic living moving intelligence. When I invoked "above" in ritual, I asked for the wisdom of the stars; I felt enlightened by them. Filled by them. Loved by them. I saw the patterns of the stars as the Divine Order; there was sacred geometry. I wanted these sacred patterns on my body, so I sewed the designs of a few constellations on some clothing, using crystal sequins for the stars. On a deep- blue velvet dress I sewed Cygnus, the swan. Cygnus forms a huge triangle in the sky, in the Milky Way. When I looked up at her, she became my portal.

I felt enveloped by the stars, enveloped like a cloak, empowered, directed, and aligned by their cosmic design. As I lay and looked at them, it was as if my inner self was undergoing a chiropractic adjustment, as if things were out of balance, disarrayed in my deepest personal self. As if the stars, with my willingness to open to them, slowly massaged my inner self into alignment with the Divine Order. The most healing soul work that I have ever done was while sleeping outside.

Above me, stars are strewn across the rich velvet night sky. I open to them, and they fill me. I see them chatter, twinkle, trying to catch my attention, shining with a kaleidoscope of colors. They tell their own stories that I cannot seem to decipher, but my soul hears. I trust that my soul hears and remembers, feeling the beauty of the cosmic divine order displayed in sacred geometry across the sky.

Longing

Ben and I got into bed at twilight one night in late October and watched the stars come out. The Summer Triangle appeared overhead, then some of the brighter stars: Antares on the southwestern horizon, and the peeking bit of the tail of Ursa Major. As the blue of the sky deepened to a rich darkness, the Milky Way showed herself, stretching across the sky with Cygnus across her midsection like a giant vulva, a swan diving toward Earth. It was wonderful to see her overhead so early. In the deep blackness of the night after the new moon, she was so bright. And the cold nip of winter air was bringing the brightness of the stars to their peak. Ophiucus was there, a large constellation located around the celestial equator, holding the serpents. In the western part of the sky, the shaman seemed to loom large, the circle of the shaman's body made up of the unfathomable dark night.

I awoke at 5:00 a.m. I looked up and saw Orion above, and the Milky Way was gone. She had set. I felt a profound sense of loss and loneliness, a sense of being unprotected, a sense of being on a lit path that is suddenly plunged into a deep darkness. I began to feel that this was the way of winter.

But in the winter night sky, Ursa Major shows in full. During the summer, she seems tipped at an odd angle, and she does look more like a pan, indeed a big dipper, than a bear. But this October morning she was fully a bear. In my sight, she transformed from a kitchen implement to a huge magickal presence. Her front and back claws were glistening little stars, her face distinct, her body filling the sky. Her presence was palpable. This for me is the winter sky. I look to the mother bear in the winter sky for what I look for with the Milky Way in the summer sky. But I miss the comforting presence of the Milky Way.

Kalli Rose once told me, "Anne, the stars are up there in the daytime as well. Just because you can't see them, doesn't mean they aren't there."

Oh. Of course.

If I open my mind and heart, I can see them. I can feel them.

Predators and Prey

Patricia told me before I moved to the temple that there were lots of birds. We had always allowed our six cats to roam outside during the day, and Patricia was worried that they would scare off the birds. There was no reason to worry. Rachel, the only hunter of the bunch, proved to be far more interested in rabbits than birds. Sometimes one of the less motivated cats would pick a dead bird from the ground and prance around proudly. Closer inspection proved that the desiccation was rather pronounced. We weren't fooled.

When we first moved in, we were visited by a very curious roadrunner. It would pop up on the landing next to the back porch and peek in through the screen, checking us out, with long stiff tail feathers moving slowly up and down. This slow, methodical tail movement gave the roadrunner the appearance of deep concentration. One day, as the cats took a midday nap, the roadrunner trotted around the old goat barn that we had converted to a pen for the cats, curiously poking in corners, tail moving up and down when it found something interesting. The cats, never on guard, were nonplussed. The roadrunner, having sized them up and put them in the category of nonthreatening fat cats flattened by the heat, went on its way.

The ravens were similarly unconcerned, just more vocal

about it. Rachel, our lone hunter, seemed fascinated by the ravens. One day I saw Rachel in a staring contest with a raven. The raven squawked wildly, but kept its eyes locked on our cat. The cat and bird were about the same body size, minus the wings. I wondered if Rachel was strategizing. Then another raven flew down, creating a squawking duet. Defeated but not showing it, Rachel leaned over, put her back leg in the air, and began cleaning her inner thigh with a decided air of nonchalance. The ravens hopped around, the standoff complete. Draw or détente?

Summer and winter, the screened-in porch on the west side of the house was one of our favorite places. We started out with chairs and a table, enjoying meals and evenings there. Then we bought a futon so that we could sleep there as an alternative to the Starbed, especially on the occasional rainy night or when the bright light of the full moon hindered sleep. From the porch we had a stunning view of the western sky, the low mountains to the south and north, and a clear view of the horizon to the west. We curled together to watch the sunsets turn from intense orange to the muted violets of dusk, followed by the white points of the brightest stars in the darkening sky.

We continued Patricia's tradition of having bird feeders in the mulberry tree right outside the porch. I added a goldfinch feeder, and we were highly entertained watching them feed upside down. The tree vibrated in the morning with the motion of the chickadees, house finches, and sparrows. The birds would fly from the tree to the feeder to the bank of creosote bushes nearby, circling round and round, and the tiny yellow flowers on the creosote bobbed when they landed. Ravens and hawks and, on their seasonal visits, vultures and turkey buzzards, perched in the two towering cottonwoods to the south and the north.

Under the mulberry tree, we placed a large bowl of water with a rock in the center as a bird bath. The birds loved it, sitting on the edge and sipping or hanging out on the rock. Smaller cottontail and the cartoonishly large jackrabbits would come by the bowl, their little front paws gripping the edge, and lean in to drink. They would stop by sometimes in the morning for a drink, but most often they congregated at dusk. At night we would hear rustling in the dark as larger animals—coyotes and bobcats—came by to drink. Sitting on the back porch, we were entertained from dawn until late into the night.

Things went well at the bird feeding station. Plenty of customers, lots of variety, only a few scuffles now and again. Dawn and dusk were accompanied by the cacophony of birdsong.

The Goldfinch and the Bullfrog

On one of her frequent retreats at the temple, Abbi McBride, a fellow priestess from Las Vegas, went to the spring for a bit of meditation and communion. She came back with a remarkable tale.

While she sat on the bank, contemplating life, two goldfinches flew to the edge of the water. One drank a little, and then flew onto the limb of one of the young cottonwoods, one of the Three Sisters. The other goldfinch was out of Abbi's view, but had stayed near the edge of the spring. Abbi sat enveloped by the divine beauty of these bright golden birds, listening to them chat, each call followed by a response. Suddenly, she heard a loud splash. She stood up and looked down to the water, where she saw a large circle rippling outward, sloshing on the opposite bank. The goldfinch in the tree called to its mate. Silence. The bird called plaintively, repeatedly. But there was only silence and the slow stilling of the water as the ripples melted lower.

Thus, the tales of the bird-eating monster living in the spring began. And they grew with each telling. And with each telling, the splash was louder, the surviving mate was lonelier. And the final silence was deeper.

We discovered later that bullfrogs eat birds. In fact, bullfrogs will also eat other bullfrogs.

Red-tail Feathers

A red-tailed hawk family moved into one of the cottonwoods overlooking the house. We saw them now and again, rustling up at the top of the tree. One hot Monday afternoon, Ben and I decided to drive into town for a dinner and movie date. When we walked out to the car to leave, we saw the body of a bird in the gravel of the driveway. The feathers were dappled black and white. The body was completely still. We stood in silence for a moment.

Then it moved, but only slightly.

We surmised that this juvenile male red-tail had flown into the glass window on the side of the house and fallen on the ground with a massive concussion. We waited and kept watching, making sure our cats didn't see this as an easy moment of glory. Watching this hawk try to stand was, well, rather comical. He finally got to his feet, weaving like a drunk and teetering close to falling, then regained his stance. He did this for quite a while, shaking his head as if trying to regain his composure. Then, suddenly, he flew away.

A couple of mornings later, Ben and I were sitting with morning coffee and tea out on the back porch when the young red-tail swooped from high above in the tree and flew to a creosote bush. It seemed as though he was saying hello, letting us know he was okay. A few days later, when I was walking under the cottonwood where the red-tails made their home, I heard a rustle. I looked up to see the mother red-tail sitting on a branch.

She dropped a beautiful tail feather right in front of me. I was overwhelmed with gratitude at this gift.

One afternoon Ben came into my office bursting with excitement. He had been sitting on the screen porch, telephone in hand and headset on during a teleconference with work, when a hawk shot down out of the tree, grabbed a small dun-colored bird on the ground, and flew away. As truly amazed as only an aerospace engineer can be, he described the lightning speed of the hawk diving straight to the ground and at the last minute swooping up with prey in talons.

Only a few days later, while sitting on the back porch together, we suddenly saw a speeding shape plummet straight for the earth, grab an unsuspecting tiny bird in its iron beak, then fly swiftly away with dinner in hand—or rather, mouth. Ben had not been exaggerating. It was fast.

It was an amazing feat. It was also violent, ruthless, and shocking. The scene touched something deep, limbic, in my brain—and left me shaken.

It was heartrending to know that we were feeding all these small birds at our feeders, only to have them be hunted by an impossibly swift and accurate predator. Our paradise had been shattered. Well, my untutored vision of paradise had been shattered. The beautiful moment that I had shared with the baby hawk, carefully watching until he recovered, and the glorious gift of the feather from the mother could only have happened because there were smaller birds to eat. Of course, I would have preferred that the hawks eat the mice. Much as I loved the cute little mice, the mess they left in our kitchen cupboards was disgusting and infuriating. But the birds! The little birds had done nothing but entertain us. Obviously, this cycle was not about me, or what I thought was cute.

Everything is food for something else. We are food for the earth. The earth is food for us. Let me think deeply on that for a minute. I am food. I am food for lions. I am food for ravens. I am food for flies. I am food for bacteria. Does harmony, does paradise mean that no one is food for any-one else? Obviously, it can't. Life is sustained by other life. Do I see myself as a willing contributor to life for someone else? Can I be a willing contributor to the life of a fly as it eats my desiccating flesh? Can I give that lovingly? How can I expect to receive the benefits of life, the lives of all the plants and animals that I consume every day, if I am not willing to give myself? I can be willing to give up my body after I'm dead to be eaten. But I flinch at the idea of a swift predator coming out of the sky and grabbing me in her mouth. I am priestess to a goddess who is half woman and half lioness, one of the largest predators on Earth. I need to embody both predator and prey to feel the cycle.

Journey to the Tree

On this journey, Sekhmet meets me right away. I am surprised because I have not called her or looked for her. But, there she is. She shows me a tree, and I realize it is the mesquite in front of our house. In ordinary reality, the tree is long dead, and in death, it is a beautiful sculpture. Its branches pattern against the sky in lovely lines, and Ben has fashioned a cactus and rock garden around it. It has become the centerpiece of our courtyard.

But in my journey, Sekhmet shows me this tree, and it is alive. I sit with Sekhmet and watch the tree, and as I gaze within, I realize I am the tree. I feel the rush of life, the greening of my leaves, my roots as they search for water, find it, and grow. I grow, taller and taller, wider and wider. My roots push deep underground, farther and farther, searching for more water.

I feel myself move through seasons. Spring is heady. I am intoxicated with growth energy, feeling the push as new leaves sprout. As the heat rises, I conserve water, still pushing my roots downward, in search of more. At fall I feel the release of letting it all go, and I sleep through winter. I live this life for years and years.

At some point, I feel thirsty again. I try to push my roots farther down, but realize that I am not as strong as I used to be. I begin to know the feeling of weakness. Even when spring comes around, it isn't the same rush. I don't feel the invincible strength that had surged through me before. I can barely push my roots down. The water seems to be receding, and I try to push and reach it. The land feels dry. And I feel weak. I can no longer push.

I begin to die. I feel myself dying. I know it. I can feel the tips of my limbs drying out. I try to push my roots to water, but I cannot. I try to suck water through them, and nothing happens. I can't even feel the ends of my roots. I panic. I am really and truly dying.

I feel trapped, trapped in a dying shell. Before, my trunk had been a source of growth and strength; now my trunk is a jail cell, and I am imprisoned with no chance of release. I can sense people around me every now and then, I can hear their voices. Someone carelessly snaps off a twig, and I know I am dead to them. I cry out, cry out to that person, asking them to be careful, to be respectful, that I may look dead but that inside, inside this trunk, I am alive. No one hears.

But I don't drift off into sleep, I don't slowly die on the inside. I stay alive, panicking, and helpless on the inside while my outside dies. It is horrific. More voices, people coming and going, treating me like a dead thing, when in fact I am alive on the inside, I am ensouled. But no one knows. I am just another dead thing in the desert.

And as I hear voices close by, I feel my limbs being torn and cut down. I feel my body being taken apart. I scream, I cry, but no one hears. I know they think I am dead, but I'm not! I am alive, trapped inside this dead trunk! I am hysterical, panicking, screaming. But no one hears, and my limbs are cut off. My trunk dismembered.

I sit in the ground, a small live consciousness deep within something dead. How long will I live like this? Life trapped in death? Can this go on for eternity? It is too bleak to even contemplate. I try to curl up and forget, forget who I am, what I am. I try to disappear from this nightmare. I stay this way for a long, long time.

Until I feel drops of water.

Little drops of water, splashing on me. I can't even turn over, open my eyes, or wake up fully. But somewhere, somehow, I recognize the feel of the water. And it feels so good.

The little drops keep coming, day after day. And slowly, very slowly, I come to, my awareness stretching, bit by bit. The water drops reviving me, bit by bit.

I hear voices. Fuzzy at first, but at some point I recognize a voice. It is Ben. And I can see him, holding a green watering can and carefully tending the cactus around me. He comes over and gives me a little more water, this dried stump. And I can feel his hope, his love, his generosity. With the water and his love combined, and I breathe in life.

That was the end of the journey. I sat next to Sekhmet as we watched Ben water the dried stump, seeing his love and hope so palpable. I looked over at her, questioning. What was I supposed to get from this journey? Did I need to move to political action, becoming involved in water rights and conservation? Should this journey move me to environmental action? She looked at me, straight in the eye. *This journey is to teach you what it is to be a tree. What it is to die. That is the lesson you need now.*

I think about this journey frequently. I think about it when I turn on the water faucet, bringing my consciousness to everything that depends on water for life. I think about it when I see dead trees, wondering if, like me, they contain a consciousness trapped, scared. I think about it every time we cut wood for the temple fires, knowing that even when we take only the trees that seem completely dead, they may not be dead. We honor the trees with ceremony before we cut, and I connect with their consciousness during the ritual, asking if we can cut, hearing their answers.

As I grow older, I think about this journey and my own body, knowing that I might feel trapped within it. I think about this journey as I volunteer with hospice patients, especially those in a comatose state. I think about this journey when I am with Ben, showered with his love, generosity, and hope. And I am grateful for the blessings of this life.

Still Life with Rabbits

Our first winter at the temple, we were inundated with rain. By the next spring, we were flooded with rabbits. Colonies of them scampered through the yard, congregating without regard for their different species.

The jackrabbits stood tall above the rest, long ears towering.

The black marks on the tops of their ears reminded me of feather markings, and indeed they did look like they were wearing two very large feathers. These beasts were lanky, almost ungainly when they sat upright and comical when they walked. If they went just a short distance, they would lean over and put out their skinny-armed front paws first, then their oversized powerful back legs would hop forward. But when they bounded through the desert, they were the epitome of grace and beauty. When we took our morning walks, the jackrabbits would appear out of nowhere and leap away from us. They would take a number of smaller jumps and then catch air on a giant leap, sometimes saucily kicking up their back legs.

In comparison, the cottontails were diminutive, Easter-bunny rabbits. Small, round, and brownish, they blended perfectly with the desert palette, except for their bright white cottontail. Not very many white things were found in this desert, so the bright white spot on these rabbits was a beacon that could be seen from ground level. I can only imagine how obvious they would be from above. But I'm sure a predator or two was as surprised as we were sometimes to see jackrabbits among the cottontails. The first time I saw one, I thought I had been out in the desert too long, but indeed, there they were in the desert reference book.

One afternoon while sitting on the porch, I watched a cottontail over by a creosote bush munching at some dried desert brush. Suddenly a red-tailed hawk swooped down from high in the cottonwood, her shadow running across the ground near the cottontail. The rabbit sat perfectly still, not moving. I watched in amazement as I had rarely seen any creature stay so very still. I kept watching, thinking that the hawk was gone and so the rabbit would move on, but she stayed right there, frozen. I went back to my reading but kept looking up, and she remained there, still not flinching.

She sat there for over a half an hour, never moving. I got bored waiting for her to move, and I suppose any predator would as well. Half an hour is a long time. And then she suddenly bounded away. I gained a new respect for the rabbits, seeing them as not just cute little creatures hopping around the desert and flashing their white fluffy tails, but careful and clever, with the resilience to wait out the predator. I saw how defenseless they were, with soft fur and stubby claws. Their only defense was speed. And if they didn't have a head start, they were doomed. I sat and ruminated on the feeling of being prey, of being defenseless. I remembered the time in a taxi in Guatemala when I felt defenseless, the driver taking me through back roads and away from help. I remembered the time I was raped on a date in college, my beer-fueled haze impeding my ability to cope but not dulling my sense of helplessness.

I am the priestess of a goddess who is half woman, half lioness. I am the priestess of a goddess whose well-told myth casts her as the predator, destroying the human race. I am the priestess at a temple dedicated to peace, built a few miles from the nuclear explosives testing site. I am a woman who has been helpless. I am a woman who lives each day on the lives of other beings, with every bite. I am a priestess of Sekhmet, she who is both woman and lion.

Peace and Activism

The temple sits serenely in the crosshairs of modern warfare. The F-15s, F-16s, and A-10s roar overhead, lining up their landing approach with the seven-petal lotus of the temple dome. Bombs explode at irregular intervals, some a distant *whomp* and others terrific explosions that rattle the windows of our house, their sudden booms causing me to once drop a glass I was washing in the sink. The Air Force demonstration team, the Thunderbirds, practices in the skies over the temple. They fly menacingly low, causing me to feel powerless in the face of their feats, at their mercy, dominated. They are super-human; they can squash me at any moment. I am a weak insect. I am grateful not to be the target, yet I am touched by the cold shadow of the fear felt by those who are indeed targets.

There are days when I feel irritated that the noise of the jets and bombs disrupts the serene silence of the temple and the desert. There are days when I feel a sense of terror as the jets fly over and bombs explode at seemingly close range, wondering what would happen if they missed, empathizing with those who live with these noises and knowing they are the targets. There are days when I am amazed at these jets, what they are able to do, the prowess of the pilots, the technological mastery that makes them fly and swoop like menacing black metal swallows.

There are days when I feel just plain angry at the amount of money spent on military operations, at the amount of money spent on jet fuel as the Thunderbirds practice their aeronautical acrobatics while children in Las Vegas go to bed hungry. There are days when I feel helpless and powerless in the face of my country's political decisions and the military-industrial complex. And there are days when I ignore it all, resign myself to it, and don't even think about it.

From my first night at the temple, I contemplated the twin human powers of protection and aggression, identified in the rumble of a truck's diesel engine and the growl of Sekhmet.

I am quite familiar with but always caught unaware by the nexus of political activism and spirituality. Personally, I wander among many responses: carrying signs, writing letters, withholding my taxes, baring my body, chanting daily, organizing events, sputtering incoherently, speaking intelligibly, raving, loving, and detesting. I don't know if any of these activities is the key, the one that turns the lock, the one that changes events, but for me it is important that I respond in a way that is genuine, from my heart, and with the full force of my will.

People ask me whether I think my voice helps, whether the rallies help, whether chanting for peace in my personal meditation helps, whether protesting helps. Whether any of this helps. *Help* is an interesting choice of vocabulary and an interesting concept in this context. What does it mean that something *helps*? *Help* here means, I believe, that the protests, chanting, and meditation have a direct causal relationship to *peace*. Yet in the American twin ideas of "more is better" and "instant results," sparsely attended protests and lone chanters don't seem effective.

From my perspective, I lead and participate in peace activities because I want to affirm my deep pledge to a peaceful world.

And with every chant, every action, I reinforce within myself that this is truly what I want to see, reaffirming my pledge to bring about peace within and without.

I consider peace activism as a way to "repair the web," from Carol Christ's beautifully conceived and written "Nine Touchstones of the Goddess."[25] For me, repairing the web can be as simple as the recognition and acknowledgment of others' pain and humanity. This serves to viscerally place me in the web, where the knots and cords are unmistakable, the bonds binding, and the feeling of being a thread in the interwoven whole penetrates my soul.

Ash Wednesday at the Nevada Test Site

Sometimes things seem irreconcilable, and yet coincidence creates an environment where the disparate is unified into something so beautiful that it produces a sacred light that shines on all, where, for just a flash, here on this plane, earthly concerns are released and the cosmic web of harmony is revealed. It is the moment that I see the insubstantiality of divisive elements—they are thin and transparent. In 2006, Ash Wednesday at the Nevada Test site blossomed in the beautiful sacred space of coincidence.

The Nevada Test Site is a mere twenty minutes north of the temple on Highway 95. On the south side of the highway with a glorious view of the surrounding desert lies Peace Camp. Peace Camp was the site of mass peace and anti-nuclear demonstrations in the 1980s, including the "Reclaim the Test Site" protest in March of 1988 with over eight thousand demonstrators and two thousand arrests. Protests continued, including the Mother's Day demonstration of 1988 with over ten thousand protestors. After the "Reclaim the Test Site II" protest in 1989, the authorities bulldozed Peace Camp in May of 1989 and evicted

thousands of protestors. When Genevieve purchased the land
and had the temple built, it was a safe haven for the protestors.
Peace Camp is still used for protests, including a Mother's Day
Reunion demonstration in May of 2008. Annually, the Newe
hold a spirit walk/run ending at Peace Camp.

On the north side of the highway is the test site. Skinny
barbed-wire fence roams through the desert parallel to the
highway, ending at the heavily fortified gate that spans the road
leading to the test site. Past the gate are two open-air pens used
to imprison activists who are arrested for acts of civil disobedi-
ence, the most common act being crossing the line at the gate
into the restricted territory.

We met at the Nevada Test Site for the Ash Wednesday
ecumenical ritual. The gathering was organized by Sister Megan
Rice, whose credentials included being arrested at countless
demonstrations, including one at the Western Hemisphere
Institute for Security Cooperation (formerly the School of the
Americas).[26] She worked with Nevada Desert Experience, a
group that promotes faith-based peace actions. A dozen or so of
us gathered on a Christian holy day, an unlikely congregation
of spiritual leaders hailing from Christian, Native American,
Goddess Pagan, Huna (Hawai'ian), and Humanist backgrounds.
We were separated by dogma but united for peace. Sister Megan
asked us each to lead a prayer.

We gathered near the gate, an area long accustomed to
demonstrations and actions. The sapphire sky glistened, a light
breeze blew, and the radiant warmth of the sun embraced us. A
bird chirped nearby, circling us overhead then flying over the
barbed-wire fence onto the test site. Not fearing arrest, the bird
chirped noisily, calling to us from the restricted side.

Corbin Harney prayed a powerful prayer in his native Newe
language. The earth at the Nevada Test Site knew Corbin, and

this relationship was palpable. I felt the Earth spirit rush up to meet him, reveling in the communion of their two spirits. We stood in awe as he prayed for peace. As I felt the spirit of the Earth answer his call, I yearned for that relationship.

Earlier that morning I had lit candles and some frankincense in the temple, readying myself for this ceremony at the test site. In the temple Sekhmet sits facing north, facing the test site. In the temple I sat in front of her, both of our faces turned to the test site, chanting and praying for strength and understanding.

The group turned to me, and I lit the frankincense. I turned north, feeling Sekhmet at my back, my red dress whipping in the wind and incense smoke gliding to the sky. I held my head high and raised my voice to her, reciting her one hundred names. I felt her, the Protector of the Divine Order. Her roar echoed across the desert. I reveled in her presence, reveled in my relationship with this goddess.

A Huna priest led a ceremony of moving into "right relationship" with the Earth. We each made our apologies to the Earth and then we all repeated a phrase about righting our relationship with the Earth: "Dearest Mother Earth, I apologize for thoughtlessly using your resources for gratification instead of nurturance. Help me to know the difference."

In honor of Ash Wednesday, Sister Megan suggested that we take a bit of earth from the ground and mark ourselves with it, saying "I am the Earth." The remains of a campfire that Corbin had built for his annual Sunrise ceremony on New Year's Day were nearby, and we used the ashes to mark ourselves. I put the ash on my throat, signifying my commitment to speak about the test site.

After our prayers, we anointed one another with water pooled from the rain on a previous day, and Corbin playfully anointed me with a mischievous smile that said, "Tag, you're it."

I brought a sage wand that had been left at the temple in front of Madre del Mundo by a peace activist on her way to California, and we smudged.

It was a beautiful weaving of traditions and seemingly irreconcilable threads. I left with a renewed sense of action re-igniting my dedication to chanting for peace.

I began concluding our ceremonies at the temple with a chant for peace that I had fashioned using various sources including a Sanskrit *shanti patha* and the Newe word *Shundahai*, meaning "peace and harmony with all creation." Every time I heard Corbin intone the word *Shundahai*, my heart opened and I felt a deep connection with the land, with all of creation. I imag-ined the chant given life by many voices and projected through the dome of the temple, amplified by the crystals within the cop-per tubes, sailing with the wind, reaching ears far away with a whisper of peace:

> May all know Peace. Peace, only Peace.
> May the Skies know peace.
> May the Earth know peace.
> May the Waters know peace.
> May the Plants know peace.
> May the Trees know peace.
> May all know peace. Peace, only Peace.
> And may that Peace come to me.
> Shundahai, Shundahai, Shundahai.

During one peace action at the Nevada Test Site, a man approached me and asked, "Does this really help?" Yes, that question again. And my honest answer was and still is, *I don't know.* I don't know if it helps or what form it might take—if help means action will be taken by the federal government directly motivated by my protest. But what I do know is that chanting for peace brings me into the cycle, it makes me aware every day that there are places, people, hearts, and souls that do not know peace. My chants may be whispers on the winds, but they are consistent whispers. I keep chanting to bring myself to the awareness of peace and to breathe life into the idea, the reality, of peace. And I chant for the strength of the lioness, the strength of Sekhmet, to embody peace.

One hot summer afternoon, a woman came to the temple. She was a lifelong peace activist and had fallen in love with a pilot from the National Guard. She had come to the temple to find guidance and direction. We made a fire together and burned sage that had been picked and bundled by Willy, another peace activist and war veteran. We sat on the sun-warmed stones, the flames absorbing her words, healing and transforming. She cried and prayed, wondering how to honor this beautiful man whom she loved and his deep commitment to protect his family and country, how to honor that soulful sentiment and remain firm in her peace activist stance. I left her in silence.

There Are No Words

At noon on a bright and cool day in April 2005, two busloads of people arrived at the temple. These were not ordinary Pagan tourists but a Japanese peace delegation that had come to Nevada to protest nuclear testing. They stopped at the temple for a picnic after touring the Nevada Test Site.

Earlier in the week, they had visited the atomic testing museum in Las Vegas, a museum devoted to the glorification of nuclear testing. The mushroom cloud, a sight which must have evoked fear, misery, and despair for the Japanese visitors, is available on key chains and mousepads.

The group numbered over sixty—ranging in age from late twenties to mid-seventies. One of the older men had obvious signs of radiation disfigurement, one side of his face scarred. As I looked at him, he smiled, and I returned his easy smile with my own, while my mind spun with increasing feelings of pain, anger, and guilt.

I led them to the temple, where they immediately organized a group picture. They brought me gifts of peace—peace cranes, books explaining the atrocities of the bombing of Nagasaki and Hiroshima, cards, a statue, pins, and leaflets. I told them about Genevieve Vaughan's dedication to the peace movement. They asked me if the dome of the temple was modeled after the A-bomb dome.[27] My lame answer of a mumbled "not sure" brought me to the full realization of how little I knew about the bombings at Nagasaki and Hiroshima.

We all returned to the guest house grounds to eat lunch. After lunch, they presented me with more gifts and donations for the temple. They boarded their air-conditioned tour buses amid smiles, bows, and waves. I realized that only a couple of them had actually spoken any English to me, yet I felt the unspoken communication of their presence. While they visited, of course, I was caring for their needs, making sure everyone had hot tea, a place to sit, and enough food. When they left, I sat and reflected on the day's happenings.

I looked over the books and leaflets graphically portraying the horrors of the bombings at Nagasaki and Hiroshima. The dead bodies. The live bodies ravaged by radiation. The destruction and the pain. These were the relatives of the people included in the afternoon's delegation. These were the people in the delegation.

I went to the temple and knelt in front of Sekhmet, a goddess attributed with destroying humanity. I prayed to her because she knows the price of destruction. I said her hundred names, chanted her chants. She is the mother of the gods. She is primeval. She is creation. I sat with her, irritated by my inability to cognitively understand her mysteries and overwhelmed psychically and physically by them.

I cry for Norb, a longtime peace activist who died after the Easter Peace Walk with Nevada Desert Experience. On the final morning, approaching the test site, he had stumbled and fallen. His head bloodied, he refused treatment and continued toward the gates, holding his peace banner high. That was his last demonstration. I cry for the Japanese delegation, handing me their cranes, bowing in mutual respect. I cry not only for what I do not understand but also for what I cannot change. I cry for the responsibility of being American. I cry for the strength, perseverance, and love of the protesters I meet. I cry until nothing at all is clear. On this bright April day, I feel the horrors of the past. And I cry.

Is this what helps? Does it help to feel the contours, the rents, the sharp edges, the frayed ends of the web? Does it help to taste both the sweet and acrid layers? Is this the mystery, dear Sekhmet? How do I begin to understand aggression and destruction in the name of protection? How do I know my own anger? I feel the courage and love of your beating heart and the strength and tenacity of your lethal claws. I sit with creation and destruction, paired and united.

Living the Mysteries of Sekhmet

During my three years of living at the temple, I lived outside of the Christian American calendar, celebrating the turn of the seasons and undulating with the cycle of the moon. Truly living "as above, so below; as the universe, so the soul; as without, so within," I basked in the revolutions of the sun; the waters of my body ebbed and flowed with the cycle of the moon. I opened myself to the stars and planets of the cosmos every night, watching their procession across the sky and feeling the changes each wrought. I understood finally what it meant to embody spirituality, to embody my spiritual practice, to live it for myself, and to lead others through the cycles of the seasons. This was natural, easy, and I surrendered to it gratefully and with an open heart.

Then there was Sekhmet. How could I live, embody, and lead her mysteries? How could I make sense of a deity accused of destroying the world, who was sedated by alcohol to bring her out of her fury? And, to add a further layer of incongruity, how could I embrace the idea that a deity who is often called a warrior, often associated with war, resides here at a temple, proudly standing as a testament to peace?

People would come to the temple and expect me to be able to explain Sekhmet. I would invite them to come chant with me, say her names. I told them the myth of "The Destruction of Humanity." I told them the history of the temple. The incongruities stood stark. I'm sure many people considered me an airheaded goddess worshipper who was too deep in her New Age hoo-ha to figure out that this didn't make sense. People will think what they will.

But I wanted to understand—for myself. I wanted to write poetry to Sekhmet just as the priestess Enheduanna had written poetry in honor of Inanna 4,000 years ago.[28] I wanted to hear the poetry read and sung in her honor. But to do that, I needed to "get it." And I needed to get it bone deep.

I went many routes to discover these answers, and hoped that by sinking fully into them all I could clear the cognitive dissonance that pervaded my thoughts. One route led me through the aisles of academia, digging through books and journal articles. Another route led me through my interactions with those who came to honor her at the temple—what did Sekhmet mean to them? What did she help them with? How did they perceive her? Another route led me through myself. I met her in trance journeys. I met her in ritual. I continued to pay homage to her, chant her name, arrange festivals in her honor, always listening and feeling her. I began to surrender gratefully to her mysteries.

Myths

The first place that goddess researchers usually go to understand a deity is to the myths. Goddesses who are honored in living religions like Buddhism, Hinduism, and Yoruba have a continued tradition practiced today that links with their ancestral roots. The myths of these goddesses continue to be told in contemporary times. In order to research goddesses like Sekhmet who are part of ancient traditions not practiced in a continuum to the present, we need to look at how these goddesses were worshipped and honored in their ancient context. That posed particular problems for me. First, I did not have an academic background in Egyptian studies, so I could only rely on secondary sources and translations. This meant that I was always looking through someone else's eyes—eyes that were not looking for the same thing I was. In my academic research on Mesoamerican goddesses, my knowledge of Spanish and Nahuatl had shown me time and time again that translations were not full enough to deliver the nuances of narrative, and that in reading papers and books solely in English, usually by American scholars, I learned only a shadow of the full story.

Taking into account my limited investigative skills, relying on secondary sources and translations, I researched everything I could regarding the myths of Sekhmet, her names, the stories that were told about her by those who worshipped her, and which cultures called her names in prayer and why. I was fortunate enough to find Normandi Ellis's works, as she is both an academic researcher and a spiritual practitioner. I wanted to read about Sekhmet from the perspective of someone academically informed who sees her as a divine entity, who experiences her in multiple ways, and who believes in her.

There are relatively few myths mentioning Sekhmet, and the ones that do mention her as the Eye of Re, the Eye of the Sun. In Egyptian mythology, the Eye of the Sun is a personage, a character that represents the concentrated and directed strength of the sun. Three myths about the Eye interweave and overlap, sharing characteristics and differences. They are all found in different texts, so they should not be seen as linear or congruent; however, these stories do provide an interesting and fuller portrait of The Eye and Sekhmet. In the first two myths, The Eye leaves Egypt. The Eye creates humanity in the first myth and sets out to destroy humanity in the third. The Eye's return to Egypt in the second and third myths is heralded with fanfare and joyous festivities.

In the first of these three myths, the version from *The Book of Smiting Down Apophis*, the Eye leaves Egypt and follows the deities Tefnut and Shu. Upon her return, the Eye is enraged to find that Atum-Re created another Eye to take her place. Her tears of rage and grief form human beings. Atum-Re then places the Eye on his forehead as the uraeus, where it rules over everything.[29]

In the second myth, often referred to as "The Distant Goddess," The Eye leaves Egypt and goes south to Nubia. Re realizes that he is powerless without his Eye, so he sends an emissary to convince the Eye to return. Through much storytelling, cajoling, and charm, the Eye is persuaded to return. Upon the Eye's return, everyone rejoices and a great festival is given in her honor.[30] According to one text, upon return the Eye "has come to rest and has stopped in Isheru in her form of Sekhmet."[31] The Eye can be seen as the first feminine being, and the ensuing festival upon her return (in both this and the third myth) was celebrated as "the welcoming of a beneficial force for all of Egypt."[32]

The third myth, the one most commonly associated with Sekhmet, is referred to as "The Destruction of Humanity," and is from *The Book of the Heavenly Cow* found on the walls of royal Egyptian tombs from the nineteenth and twentieth dynasties, around 1200–1100 BCE. This myth is considered to be one of the oldest ancient Egyptian narratives.

The "Destruction of Humanity" myth opens with a group of humans rebelling against Re, the aging solar god. Re brings together a council of elder deities for advice. Among those attending is his Eye, who created humans. Nun, the primeval chaos, suggests that Re send his Eye out to wage war against the humans who rebelled against his authority. The Eye, in the form of the goddess Hathor, goes to slay the human rebels, who have fled to the desert. She slaughters the rebels and then returns to

Re, saying that she "overpowered mankind, and it was agreeable
to my heart." And it is here that "Sekhmet came into being."
Considering this, Re decides that he does indeed want to rule
over the humans.

Realizing that Sekhmet will destroy the rest of humanity,
Re has a change of heart. He commands his chief priest to grind
red ochre to mix with seven thousand jars of barley beer being
brewed by women. On the eve of Sekhmet's planned destruction
of humanity, the intoxicating draught is completed and poured
into the fields where she will arrive. In the morning, Sekhmet
arrives to find the fields brimming with the red beer. Seeing her
own reflection in the flooded plains, she is delighted and drinks
her fill. She is then too intoxicated to even recognize humans.
Re greets her with the words "Twice welcome in peace, O
Charming One" and decrees that every year women will brew
intoxicating draughts for a great feast in her honor.

Variants of "The Destruction of Humanity" story exist in
Egyptian mythology with different deities and different rebel-
lions, which cause this narrative to be viewed as a repeating
pattern of events.[33] The myth shares many similarities with other
myths that depict deities creating humans and then ultimately
destroying them because they were dissatisfied with their creation. This supports the principle that a deity that is powerful
enough to create life is also powerful enough to destroy it. And
in this ancient Egyptian myth, that power resides with female
deities. The power of Sekhmet is beyond the male gods' control;
she is a force of nature, wild and indiscriminate.

In all of these myths, the Eye is a symbol of power, the
awesome and awe-full power of the sun. This power spans the
destructive acts of creation and the creative acts of destruction.

Ancient Egyptians reenacted the myth of "The Destruction
of Humanity" in an annual festival held in the first month of

the year after the flooding of the Nile. These feasts are well-documented at the temple of Mut during the reign of Hatshepsut and well into the Ptolemaic era. The temple inscriptions reveal continual singing, dancing, drinking, and music-making as acts of propitiation of Mut in her form as Sekhmet.[34]

This New Year's festival occurred after the hottest days of summer had finally ended, the rains arrived, and the Nile flooded. Ochre-colored beer, brewed by women, flowed in an ecstatic ritual of propitiation to the power of the female divine.[35] The flooding of the Nile brought the promise of the continuation of life in an annual cycle. The early floods would flush more clay, silt, and sand down the river, creating rich and fertile sediment. With the mythic identification of the Nile and menstruation, this festival honored the power of the female in all aspects.[36]

The regeneration of the land and the continuation of life were intricately tied to the cycles of the Nile. If the Nile's flooding was too high or too low, cultivation was adversely affected, often resulting in severe famine. Water, as well as the sun, wielded the forces of creation and destruction.

The New Year festival was one of the principal transition periods for the ancient Egyptians. Sekhmet was invoked and propitiated as her immense power could be wielded in many directions. A recitation of a spell called "The Book of the Last Day of the Year" was performed over a piece of cloth, which was then worn as an amulet during the days leading up to the New Year. Prayers were recited to gain the protection of Sekhmet, and tokens of Sekhmet and another feline deity, Bastet, were liberally bestowed.

The clergy of Sekhmet, the "Uab," were famed as healers and surgeons. One of the few surviving ancient Egyptian medical books, the *Papyrus Ebers*, contains many spells written expressly for the use of the clergy of Sekhmet. A comprehensive knowledge of the heart and circulation was attributed to the Uab. The heart reflected the solar attributes of regeneration. Heart scarabs, placed on the chest of the deceased, manifested the revitalizing powers of the sun, aiding the transformation of the deceased. Some heart scarabs were made of carnelian; this passage from *The Egyptian Book of the Dead*, beautifully translated by Normandi Ellis, refers to the stone's regenerative and solar qualities: "Mine is a heart of carnelian...I am the phoenix, the fiery sun, consuming and resuming myself." [37]

Sekhmet was a complicated weaving with seemingly contradictory threads: warrior and healer, protector and destroyer. I needed to surrender my preconceptions to really see the whole.

Entering Her Myth

I began to have an understanding of Sekhmet in her context in ancient Egypt. But I wanted to understand her in the depths of my bones, in the depths of my heart, and in the recesses of my mind. I wanted to understand her anger, her fury, and I wanted that understanding to encompass her love, her healing, her strength, as well as the Sun, the Lion, the Snake. I wanted to move to a place where my understanding of the whole would surpass my understanding of the discrete parts.

In my most honest moments, though, I felt trepidation. Part of me was scared of her. My father had an irrational temper and his bursts of uncontrollable anger caused us all to be wary of his moods. I can definitely access my own irrational rage. It wasn't something I wanted to use, and I certainly didn't want to be on the receiving end of someone else's temper. And here I was, faced with a deity that, at least from myth, embodied anger. Righteous anger, but still anger that lashed with uncontrolled consequences.

I spoke with many people who connected with Sekhmet over issues that required rage and strength. People told me about using the anger of Sekhmet to fuel the courage to get divorced, stand up to a boss, file a lawsuit. Righteous uses of anger. I understood and accepted that, especially given her myth.

But that wasn't the way I saw her. Or I should say, that wasn't the gift she gave to me.

One warm summer night I light a fire in the temple, giving offerings to Sekhmet and my guides. I lie down on the temple floor, stones warmed by the sun. Looking at the stars through the roof, I feel the swirl of being nurtured by the sun's warmth, the splendor of the stars, the cool embrace of night, the light of the fire. I open myself to the beauty of communion with the Divine. Ben drums the path for my journey.

On this journey, Sekhmet meets me again. We are in the temple, and I am lying on the sun-warmed stones. She looks at me with her great amber eyes, lion jaws huge. She is in full lioness form, and she puts her giant paw on my chest. Wow. It is big. And the claws are massive. I looked up at her with a bit of trepidation. "Your heart, it needs to be malleable." She places her other paw on my chest and kneads. Yes, just like a cat, only a very large cat with very large paws. I look down and realize my chest is open, and she is kneading my heart.

It doesn't hurt, but I cannot help but be slightly disconcerted, seeing the large paws and claws pushing, tearing, kneading my heart. At some point, I surrender to it and allow myself to be there, in that place, and to feel it. Feel the hardness of parts of my heart. Feel the sharp

edges. Feel the places that don't yield to touch. But her
large paws knead, softening the edges and the unyielding
places in my heart.

    She stops, and I sense my heart as open, strong yet
receptive, malleable yet shaped. I sit in that moment,
aware of this sensation, knowing that with this heart I
can be courageous and loving and open all at once. But
only moments later, I feel the sharpness returning, parts
of my heart hardening. And she starts again, kneading my
heart to suppleness, openness, strength. When the knead-
ing ceases, the hardening begins again, but the time in
between has lengthened. She begins another round of
kneading, and afterward the time before the hardening
begins lengthens again. Rounds and rounds and rounds
of kneading, until finally my heart remains supple, strong,
open, and brave.

As I recall this journey, remembering that beautiful warm
evening, I feel my heart. Here at my computer, years later, I can
once again feel the hard edges of my heart. Events pass through
my mind, moments when I would not let my heart expand. I see
clearly how fear shrinks my heart to stone. And that I am braver,
stronger, more sincere, and more authentic when I trust my heart
and allow it to be open. I yearn again for a strong supple heart,
and remain in infinite gratitude that I know it is possible.

I tried to reconcile these multiple images. I wanted to
understand Sekhmet in her totality. I wanted to understand this
warrior goddess who had so lovingly and patiently massaged my
heart. I needed to understand her myth in its totality, understand
her context in the myth, understand the myth's context in its own
history as well as the present. I did not want to strip her of her
anger, her righteous rage, her strength, her drunkenness, or her

power. But the goddess of this myth was not the totality of the goddess I met in her temple.

During my first year, I read everything that I could find on Sekhmet, every little piece of writing, academic and personal. I started chanting to her. I memorized her names and began to listen for new ones. My daily practice consisted of going to the temple, lighting a fire, saying her names, chanting her mantra, letting it reverberate through my body, my heart, hoping that once my body understood, my mind would understand. Who is she? Who am I to her? What does she teach me? Day after day. Fire after fire. Offering after offering. I didn't ask for understanding. I just kept surrendering, moving beyond the fear of my mind into the knowing of my body, and the knowing of my heart.

Connecting to Her

I began chanting the Sanskrit mantra of devotion to Chinna-masta. Chanting mantras is a millennia-old tradition. The word *mantra* means instrument of thought, sacred text, or a prayer of praise. Repeating a mantra over time can calm the mind as well as spark our inner fire.

After a few months of chanting, I began to notice that at times when my thoughts would wander, I would hear Chin-namasta's mantra go through my mind. It seemed as though my mind would clutch at the words and melody of the mantra. I found I was having fewer and fewer of the unhelpful thoughts: the thoughts that whispered that I was not invited to participate in a ceremony with another group because I was not talented enough; the thoughts that whispered that I did not have the spiritual depth to be a priestess; the thoughts that I was shallow and everyone knew it and that was why only three people showed up to the Full Moon ritual. Instead, these thoughts were drowned by Chinnamasta's chant. I began to see my ego attachments in these instances; my self-importance was dinged when I was not invited, and my self-aggrandizement and pride were confronted with overwhelming evidence that my charisma was not always enough to induce hordes of people to drive an hour into the desert for a ceremony. The words of Chinnamasta's mantra exposed these whisperings for their true nature. And I began the slow process of allowing my strength to come from within.

One warm summer evening while Kalli Rose was visiting, we went up to the temple and lit a fire. We chanted to Kali Ma, with Kalli's operatic voice filling the space with love and praise. At that moment, I heard very clearly the desires of Sekhmet to have songs and praise to her, songs of love and beauty with passionate and joyful energy.

But to honor Sekhmet, what did I have? Unlike the Hindu and Buddhist traditions, which are living traditions still practicing ancient techniques, the Egyptian traditions were long unpracticed as Islam gained popularity. To learn about Sekhmet and how to honor her, the only book I had to turn to was Robert Masters' *The Goddess Sekhmet: The Way of the Five Bodies.* I was uncomfortable to be so reliant on someone else's research and to feel so blinded, so unable to dig into the academic piece. In retrospect, I see how this situation brought me to a new way of understanding Sekhmet. Though I still wanted to understand Sekhmet in her ancient guise, in her Egyptian context, I was in the unique position to understand her manifestation in the Nevada desert, to understand her in the present context. And so I went forth with what I had.

Masters was my only source for a mantra, and I wanted to honor Sekhmet by saying her mantra. I wanted to connect myself to her in the same way that I had connected to Chinnamasta. I needed to understand Sekhmet's gifts in a visceral manner. I wanted my mind to cleave to her words. So I began using Masters' mantra: *Sa Sekhem Sahu.*

Sa means the Breath of Life. It is the life force that comes into the human body at conception. The word *sekhem* is associated with power. This word has also been associated with energy, particularly the energy of Kundalini. Sekhem is the power that animates the *Sahu*; it is the power that leads one to spiritual consciousness. Sahu is the spiritual body, one of the Five Bodies of each human according to Egyptian cosmology. According to Masters, Sekhmet is associated with the awakening of the Five Bodies, particularly the Sahu. The Sahu is made conscious through spiritual practice. The awakening of the Sahu is the last stage of the integration of the Five Bodies, the final stage in becoming a Realized Human.

I had no idea if this was valid historically, or if it was valid even in the present incarnation of Sekhmet here in the Nevada desert. But I knew I had to try it and see where it took me. So I began chanting her mantra.

Her mantra filled the empty crevices between the wrinkles in my brain. Her names floated through my thoughts. I began to feel the power of my breath, and there were moments when I felt the surge of connection between my body and my spirit, the moments when I felt truly one, and at one with all.

Understanding the Sun

Many solar goddesses share the common symbols of mirrors and cats. Mirrors reflect the sun. They are miniature suns. They are also closely associated with shields, which also reflect the sun, both blinding an enemy and protecting the warrior.

Sekhmet is a solar deity, often shown with the sun above her head. She is a half lioness and half woman. Cats, big and small, are associated with the sun. The image of a cat searching through the house for the sunny spot certainly comes to mind.

The uraeus on Sekhmet's head, the snake poised to strike, harnesses the energy of the sun and strikes at her command. The energy of the sun is equal parts life and death. She embodies the harshest of truths: we cannot live without the sun, but we cannot live with untempered sun.

The sun has the energies of creator and destroyer. Consider how the sun's light literally gives the energy for life on this Earth, then take into account that the sun is a giant fire, capable of causing the total destruction of Earth. There really is no difference in creation and destruction; they are not two different cycles. For anything to be created, something must be destroyed. When anything is destroyed, something is created. One doesn't come without the other. Hold the creator and the destroyer in one hand, not two, and you begin to understand goddesses such as Sekhmet.

I see her in the sun.

Days and Nights of Silence and Fast

I wanted to rewrite her myth, or better yet, write her current myth, her current story, the story of this Sekhmet, here in the Nevada desert looking out toward the Nevada Test Site. I began this task on one auspicious New Moon ritual during my first spring at the temple. I fasted and kept silent for three days, my only words out loud being her names and her mantra, and my only writings in homage to her. I spent mornings in the temple then came back to the house to write. I took my pieces back up to the temple and read them aloud, pen in hand, listening to her. I tried to be her scribe, to get her story from her mouth.

I lay down to sleep in the temple the first night, curled up in blankets in front of her. I intended to spend the night there, but the cold kept seeping under the blankets, and soon I was shivering. I headed back to the Starbed, found Ben, and curled next to his warm body underneath all the blankets. We drifted to sleep in silence.

I felt a sense of failure. I hadn't even been able to make it through the whole night. What kind of a gnarly priestess was I? But was it my fault that I get cold easily? Each night I started out in the temple then crawled late at night into the warmth of the Starbed with Ben. We were joined in the deepest of silence—the silence of the night, the silence of ourselves. Keeping silence was a beautiful experience for the two of us. When I started talking again, it was painfully obvious to me how many useless words would spout out of my mouth daily and how I used words to communicate instead of my eyes, my hands, and my heart.

The fasting was powerful, moving me to a place of not even thinking about food, not spending the time each day to figure out meals. I began feeling out of my body in the best sense—out of time, out of place. Not tied to the physical and able to surrender to spirit. Transcendent.

So, through this time, my thoughts, my words, my breath, my body, and my heart were engaged in writing her myth. I listened. I chanted. I sat. I wrote. I rewrote.

I began to understand the idea of place and the Divine, that writing about Sekhmet here in Nevada was different from writing about Sekhmet in ancient Egypt. I needed to be with her in this context, this temple, because understanding her here and now was not purely scholarly research. Knowing exactly what she was to ancient Egyptians would not reveal her totality—it would not reflect what she was right here, right now. So I began listening so that I could hear her now.

I started to see the threads come together. I saw her in the myth of "The Destruction of Humanity." I saw her here, facing the Nevada Test Site. I felt her anger, felt its source. I understood her as a force of nature, a force that is irrational, a force that wreaks havoc, and I saw the ensuing destruction that came randomly, without judgment with no sense of fairness. I saw the human-rational paradigm clearly, our need to feel that someone is in control, most especially of the forces of nature. I surrendered to that place of no control, that place of nature and spirit—that place beyond human-defined justice.

Then I began to understand Sekhmet in a visceral way, in a way that filled my heart. I yielded to her. And I was not afraid. I was not afraid of the uncontrollable or the irrational. I was not afraid of the claws, the teeth, the strength, the anger. Instead, I was overcome by bliss in the ecstasy of communion with the Divine.

Sekhmet in Her Temple in Nevada: The Twenty-First-Century Myth

I wove another reading of her myth based on the events described in Sekhmet's ancient Egyptian myths. This new myth I created was not a translation or revisioning; it was the myth of Sekhmet in her temple in Nevada, which was purposefully placed here in the desert between a bombing range and a nuclear weapons testing facility. This is ancient understanding combined with a new myth for the twenty-first century.

There was a time when all the world lived in beautiful harmony. This was a time when animals and plants and earth and humans recognized their bonds and ties. It was a time when the web was woven tightly, without loose ends and rents. It was a time when the spirits were honored, when the Divine was recognized, and peace prevailed.

That time did pass and the people forgot their place in the web. They forgot the time when death and life were balanced. They forgot the time when none had power over the other, when all gave their lives for the greater good, and all lived for the continuation and perpetuation of all. They forgot when the strong used their power to maintain the balance. They forgot when harmony prevailed. They forgot when Maat[38] was served and her laws were abided. They forgot that there was a time when the small prevailed alongside the strong, when cubs were fed and the old were protected.

The people used the land's abundance to feed their desires. They used without thought and wasted the gifts of the land. They put themselves higher than the Great Spirits; they believed that they were the architects of the Divine Order, which changed at their whim in service of their desires. Their companions—the plants, stones, and animals—all became simply implements to quench their unabated craving. Everything was in the service of the people. Then their own young and old—the infirm, the weakest, the oddest, the least of all—became the means to support the convoluted structures that evolved to satisfy their desires. The strong survived on the resources of the weak. The Divine Order had become hideously inverted.

Sekhmet's heart roared at seeing the injustice. She was sickened at this perversion. The hubris of the people had gone too far. They were beyond the point of comprehending the consequences of their actions. The fragile and beautiful must be protected and the strong must be challenged. Fiery Sekhmet came to reestablish Maat. She came because she loved the land. She came to reestablish the divine connection. She came as a human animal, as

*a woman lion. She came as the birth and the death, the
mother and destroyer and healer. She came as the sun.*

*She prowled the Earth as the lioness, devouring all
in her sight, devouring all who forgot the Divine Order.
She tasted the blood of those who dared forget the Great
Spirits. She prowled the desert, and the hot wind was her
breath, blowing destruction. Her breath dried up the life.
Her wrath flared at what had been wrought, at the injustice on Earth. Her wrath was indiscriminate. There was
no individual judgment for those acts that had been more
egregious than others.*

*The people began to understand. They began to see
themselves as part of their great, rent web. They could
comprehend the grand connections, the tremendous
responsibilities, and the exquisite beauty. In the unyielding light of the tremendous destruction, they began to
see clearly, for it was a time when everyone viscerally
understood the web, they understood their connection to
all. As destruction hailed from all corners, none were left
untouched.*

*The people who could remember the time of harmony
went to the plants to ask for guidance for an offering,
an offering that would show the deep understanding of
the relationship between humans and Earth. Those who
remembered went to their deities and asked what they
could offer to show their understanding of the Divine
Order, what could they offer Sekhmet to express their
comprehension of the sacred web and their place within
and their sacred pact to uphold it. The plants and the
deities spoke to those who would listen, and the people
painstakingly prepared a sacred brew as an offering.*

The sacred brew was made in the color of blood to

remind all of the substance of life. They offered this brew to Sekhmet as a gift to honor their sacred connection with all and their deep understanding of the splendor and responsibilities of life. Sekhmet lapped up the brew, finally able to be at peace, knowing that all had returned to a sense of common stewardship. Peace and harmony once again saturated the land as the strong cared for the weak and the gifts of life were shared.

Can you remember? Can you remember when we would give freely for the good of all? When we could feel and know the web? When sacred holy connections were honored? When beauty was abundant and love was the binding cord? When statues gleamed and offerings were piled high? When we sang to the land and danced for the Divine?

This is my myth for the twenty-first century that calls me to live a life in recognition and honor of the sacred connections in the Divine Order. To understand Sekhmet is to understand the sun, the literal life-force of this planet. That force, so great, could also easily destroy this planet. To hold the twin powers of life and death in the understanding that each is a force that does not adhere to mere human judgments of good and evil is to understand Sekhmet. This myth moves me to remember what has been broken apart. It compels me to confront the pain of what has been rent and to find my part in the repair.

The Final Ritual:
The Heart of the Sun

My third winter solstice at the temple coincided with a new moon. After the Winter Solstice ceremony, we held a New Moon women's gathering, and Novaembre and her daughter Willeoh led us in a workshop using pendulums for divination. We paired off, and my partner and I secluded ourselves in one of my favorite retreat spots, the Womb Room, a room in the guest house decorated completely in red. That winter solstice night we snuggled into the red pillows blanketing the floor, candles lit all around. We voiced our queries and looked to the swinging of the pendulum for guidance.

When I first came to the temple I was in my mid-forties, and I knew that I wouldn't stay there until my retirement. It had not been a career move, at least not in the traditional sense. Even more importantly, somewhere inside me I knew that I did not want to overstay my time; I wanted to be willing to leave when it was another priestess's turn. I relied on divination to help make my decision. Every six months I used some sort of divination, usually Tarot cards, to determine my length of stay at the temple. They always read: stay, continue on. Until that winter solstice night.

I had never used a pendulum before, but it turned out to be easy and straightforward. Ensconced in the Womb Room, we asked each other our questions. I asked whether I should stay or go. I repeated the query a number of times in a number of ways, but the answer was sure: it was time to go.

Every year that I was at the temple, we held a Sekhmet Festival at the beginning of August. That winter solstice night, when I discovered that the time was nigh, I knew that I wanted my final Sekhmet festival to be a magnificent August ceremony for this goddess who had blessed me so profoundly.

Ritual in Honor of Sekhmet: Visioning and Re-Visioning a Ceremony

I have long been inspired by ceremonies in devotion to a deity. The Durga Puja in India, the largest modern ritual in honor of a goddess, draws millions of people for nine days to give offerings and perform ceremonies and acts of devotion.[39] The temples are spruced up, the deity statues are refinished and dressed, and the grounds are tended. I wanted to create a ceremony for Sekhmet at her temple in Nevada like this. Maybe not with millions of people, but I wanted to create a time when she was solely honored.

When I began envisioning a ceremony honoring Sekhmet, I wanted it to be a ceremony of devotion. Many modern American Pagan ceremonies are built around the idea of self-actualization, which is a much needed and worthy ritual. But I wanted this Sekhmet ritual to be all about devotion to her. If self-actualization for participants happened along the way, as it often does, well, that would be a wonderful outcome. But I was looking for a ceremony built on devotion with flowers, offerings, song, praise.

My mind filled with acts of devotion that I had seen. The statues of saints and deities carried over carpets of flower petals for Easter celebrations in Antigua, Guatemala. Statues of deities pulled by men in southern India, the cords connected to barbs in

their flesh. Deities dressed in fine clothing in India. Traditional
dancers in resplendent costumes performing for La Virgen de
Guadalupe at her Basilica in Mexico City with thousands of
candles lit in her honor and pilgrims walking on their knees
in supplication. The former cathedral at San Juan Chamula
in Chiapas, Mexico, filled with healers—the *curanderas* and
curanderos—where the sense of devotion and faith is absolutely
palpable. Rice and incense offered in exquisite ceremonies to
deities in southeast Asia. The mix of Catholic and traditional
ceremony in the church at Chimaltenango, Guatemala, with its
elaborate procession of deity statues, costumes, incense, and
song.

I wanted to create a ceremony that honored Sekhmet in all
ways—with libations, incense, flowers, offerings, song, dance,
fire. In my mind's eye I could see her being carried outside
her temple for this one day, borne on a beautiful *palanquin* by
devotees, walking a path strewn with rose petals. I imagined
priestesses in red, banners waving, frankincense and kyphi
wafting, music floating. Prayers and offerings would be from the
heart, a moment for deep devotion.

Creating Ceremony in the Twenty-First Century

Most rituals maintain their gravitas, their significance, through
their staying power. Of course, at some point all rituals were
created, but rituals gain in acceptance and prominence through
years of observance. Then how to create ceremony in the twenty-
first century, ceremony true to the hearts of the modern attendees
and still, with integrity, honoring the past?

I began by looking at dates. There are many "Sekhmet
Day" dates floating around on the Internet, but I wanted a date
grounded in something—history, astronomy, season—while still

representing her contemporary visage. I turned to Normandi
Ellis's book *Festival of Lights*, which discusses ancient Egyptian
festivals and brings them into a modern context.[40] The Inebriety
of Hathor, which centers on the myth of the Destruction of Mankind, falls in the first month of Inundation, the time when the
parched banks of the Nile would flood, bringing the sustenance
for another year of life in the desert. In this instance, Sekhmet is
certainly honored at a time of great flux and change, and at a time
of the renewing of life. Ellis places this festival on August 7th.

In the modern era, August 6th or 7th is the cross-quarter
point between summer solstice and fall equinox; it is the first
harvest and the first day of autumn. It is truly a potent time.

So, at the time of year when the heat of the sun is at its
zenith in the Nevada desert, I decided to host the temple's largest ritual in honor of Sekhmet. As the season changes from
summer to fall, as the heat builds to its grand finale, it seems a
wondrous moment to contemplate her mysteries—the mysteries
of Sekhmet as the life-bringer and the death-wielder, the mysteries of the forces and cycles of nature that are beyond the scope
of human-conceived justice. In early August, Leo is in the sky
during the day, shining through the sun, the lioness's heart-star
Regulus pulsing. Sekhmet's presence at the temple in the heat of
the noonday sun is palpable and powerful.

And a name for this twenty-first-century ritual? In the spirit
of the time of year, and in honor of this solar deity, my fellow
priestess Katlyn came up with a fitting name for the festival:
Heart of the Sun.

I wanted a group of priestesses, devotees of Sekhmet, to
help plan and lead the ceremony. It would be an opportunity for
many women to lead, and to lead together. And so we did.

Making a Schedule

How was I to put together a devotional ritual? What would it look like? What would be my template, other than my haphazard and idiosyncratic musings gleaned from other rituals? I tried to understand how her statues were used in context in ancient Egypt.

It is likely that originally there were 730 statues of Sekhmet erected at the tomb of Amenhotep III (1390–1352 BC) in Western Thebes in Egypt. Of these, 365 were of the goddess seated, and 365 had her standing. Two statues for each day of the year, one seated and one standing. When I talked to Kalli Rose about this, her mind immediately jumped to the daily solar cycle, hypothesizing that there was one statue each day for sunrise and one for sunset.

So, just as Sekhmet was honored at the time of the inundation, at the time of change, volatility, and chaos, we may interpret that she was honored at the two times per day that are the point of flux and instability, the points when day and night meet and change—sunrise and sunset.

When considering these statues of Sekhmet, so many unanswered questions came to the fore. Why were some statues standing and some seated? And how to understand the idea of the instability of the change from night to day? I wondered, as well, if instead of thinking of Sekhmet as a war goddess, we should think of her as the opposite—in a sense, as one who brings stability in times of change. Or did Amenhotep III install these statues of Sekhmet as a warning against anyone who might organize rebellion? Or did he have a personal devotion to her? Pondering these issues, I felt the uncomfortable edge of the limits of my knowledge, the limits of my scholarship; I didn't even know enough to make an educated guess.

So I pulled myself back to my original purpose—to orchestrate a ritual of devotion for *this* Sekhmet in this temple in Nevada. This ceremony was not meant to reenact ancient Egyptian rituals; rather, it would be for modern devotees of this ancient Egyptian goddess.

As I worked out the ritual timing, I settled on using pieces that, as opposed to a reconstruction, were spiritually potent, auspicious, and in the spirit of Sekhmet. As Sekhmet is a solar deity, the daily solar cycle fit, and I scheduled a ritual at each point of sunrise, solar noon, and sunset, the most important solar points of each day. However, I knew that modern Euro-Americans are not really disposed to sunrise and sunset ceremonies, much less solar noon ceremonies in the desert in early August. Few shared my enthusiasm for this schedule, but in the end everyone went along.

We held the Sekhmet Festival every year for three years. By the third year, I had the schedule worked out. The Friday sunset ceremony served as a beginning gathering, to bring us together and set our intention of devotion. The Saturday sunrise ceremony began the honoring of Sekhmet, readying the temple and her statue. At the noon ceremony we lit a solar fire in the temple. At sunset we gathered, our voices ringing out in song as Sekhmet was brought out of the temple, carried by devotees on her ornate palanquin. At nightfall, we began an all-night devotional, full of singing, dancing, and ritual. On Sunday at sunrise, Sekhmet was returned to her temple on her palanquin, festooned with flowers, and feted in every way imaginable.

Each year the ceremony was more elaborate than the last. The final year, all my dreams of a festival in homage to Sekhmet were realized.

Beginning the Ceremony: Solar Fire

The sacredness of fire is central to our ceremonies at the temple. The fire pit in the center of the temple is tended only by priest- esses. The wood used in the fire is ceremonially cut. Fire, like the sun, is a source of creation and destruction. The fire transforms the space, transforms us. For the Sekhmet ritual, I wanted a sa- cred fire that had a direct connection to her solar aspect. I wanted a solar fire, a fire lit by the sun.

To light a solar fire, we used a magnifying glass to bring the sun's light into the temple's fire pit. In that way our sacred temple fire was in all actuality our sun, our star; our fire would be powerful and beautiful on literal and symbolic levels. But starting a solar fire wasn't as easy as I thought it would be. I remembered it being easier somehow in Camp Fire Girls. I set out to start the fire by using a magnifying glass and dried leaves, but the leaves just smoldered and didn't catch fire. Then I tried with leaves and tinder, but that didn't catch either. Finally, I used the magnifying glass to light some matches underneath the tin- der. That worked well and was replicable.

One of the first solar fires I started was for a Summer Sol- stice ritual. I decided to light it at noon, when the sun was at its peak. Morganne, a fellow priestess from Las Vegas, was visiting that day, and we lit the fire together. She drummed and chanted while I held the magnifying glass, her powerfully resonant voice urging on the fire, urging the tinder to light. It is surpris- ing how long it takes to light even a match with sunlight. Try it and see for yourself. But the moment it strikes, you have the glaring light, the miniature sun, the heat, the power, the fire. It was marvelous. We whooped and cheered. Morganne returned that afternoon to Las Vegas to attend another group's Summer

Solstice ritual, taking a candle lit with the flame from our solar fire to light their sacred fire.

But I was not satisfied with using the matches as the flashpoint. Did we need a different magnifying glass? Different tinder? Dot, our fire-tender and a raven-haired glamazon whose Native American and Scottish roots sculpted her high cheekbones to exquisite perfection, took on the task of developing a solar fire method. After much trial and error, she discovered that incense would light under the magnifying glass. We began to use incense as the base of our solar fires.

For the Sekhmet Festival, we gathered at solar noon on Saturday to light the fire. A group of twenty or so were there, all chanting and drumming to bring in the fire. Dot led the ritual and brought in the solar fire. At the flash of fire, we screamed with joy and the drums went wild. Now that's the way to begin a festival to Sekhmet.

I sit on the warm stones of the temple, the sun rapidly heating the day as it approaches solar noon. I squint through the lotus yantra roof, finally closing my eyes at the sun's unrelenting brilliance. I feel the heat on my face. Yes, life and death. Warmth and sun burn. Life force and death wielder. Sekhmet's warmth and the beauty of life is so easy to embrace, so sensual. I take out my magnifying glass and concentrate the sun's warm light into a strong ray, and its white beam strikes the dried leaves, searing their edges. The smoke drifts upward, its lazy circles in sharp contrast to this lightning bolt of sun. I have to put my finger under the light, to know—yes, it is painfully hot. How do I hold these twin forces of life and death? How do I see her as both, without diminishing either?

The Procession and Pavilion

At the evening procession, Sekhmet was carried out of the
temple on an elaborate palanquin. The procession to honor her
was one of my favorite pieces of the festival.

Each year, the palanquin was remade and redecorated. The
first and second years we used a wooden box painted gold, with
poles that fit into slots at either side to carry it. The poles were
long, so that two people could fit on each side and a crew of
eight could carry her. The third year, Jen and her husband Dean
brought their prodigious talents to the project. The box was
remodeled and decorated with Egyptian motifs. Multicolored
palm fronds and an image of Sekhmet graced the sides; we
affixed glass *cabochons* and mirrors to glint in the sun and firelight. It became a work of art worthy of carrying a goddess.

I imagined carrying her over a carpet of flower petals, and
in our second year that vision became a reality. One of the devotees who came to the temple worked in the floral department of
a large casino in Las Vegas. For a month she kept the rose petals
garnered from discarded flowers. The day before the festival, I
picked up two large bags of rose petals. The flowers were laid
right before the procession began, and there was not a hint of
wind. My vision was realized, and Sekhmet was carried over a
thick carpet of rose petals.

Every year the opening of the procession was spectacular.
The first year, the procession was led by fire spinners, their
dancing flames lighting up the desert night. The second year, one
of the temple devotees from Las Vegas opened the procession
by breathing a ball of fire, just as the sun went down. The third
year, the procession was opened by two teams of lion dancers,
dancing first in honor of Sekhmet and then opening the circle.

Their heavy drums and gymnastic feats raised the fire in every person there.

In the procession, Sekhmet's way was cleared using the four elements—fire, water, air, and earth. First came the fire embodied by two women spinning *poi*. Poi, a tradition among the Hawaiians and Maoris, is very popular among performance artists. The poi itself is a ball suspended by a rope or chain. For fire poi, the ball is lit and swung from a long chain. In the darkness of night, the spinning fire creates dazzling circles of flame. After fire came the *aspergers*, sprinkling rose water.[41] Next, for air, came the incense bearers, wafting kyphi. Finally, representing earth, came the flower bearers, spreading flowers in the path. Into this consecrated path came Sekhmet, born aloft in her beautiful palanquin by priestesses and devotees.

In the procession were over a dozen priestesses in red: glorious, strong, beautiful women, chanting the praises of Sekhmet. The last year we wanted Asherah, our boa constrictor, to be part of the procession, and Jen carried her, wrapping her around her waist and over her shoulder. With Asherah and the lion dancers and the priestesses, we embodied Sekhmet as woman, lion, and snake. At the end of the procession came musicians—drummers, singers, and tambourine players. It was a feast for the senses. It was a feast for the heart.

The procession ended at the pavilion, where Sekhmet was installed in the place of honor. The pavilion was constructed and decorated for this ritual, and each year it became more elaborate and beautiful, especially under the direction of Jen's artistic eye. The open-air structure was covered with red and gold cloths, silk-dyed banners that waved in the breeze. Kyphi filled the air all night.

The circle for the ritual was cast by three generations of

priestesses and devotees to Sekhmet: our priestess Novaembre,
her daughter Willeoh, and her granddaughter, Sunflower.[42] The
directions were called, loud and strong, by seven priestesses,
invoking seven aspects of Sekhmet. All of these pieces of the
ritual, eclectic and syncretic as they were, were performed with
open hearts in devotion to this deity who chose to have a twenty-
first-century home in the Nevada desert.

Night of Devotion

The night of the festival was full of devotion. We began with
reciting her names. The first year, I wore a Sekhmet mask I had
made, and I performed the recitation of her names, my voice
carrying through the desert. The next two years, we went around
the very large circle of people, each saying one of her names. We
were surrounded by her aspects, her many features manifesting
in harmony. The priestesses recited the hymn I wrote to honor
Sekhmet, telling her story. Ana, a Sekhmet devotee who traveled
annually from the East Coast to attend the festival, bespelled
everyone with her devotional songs to Sekhmet.

   Throughout each night of my last festival, everyone had
the opportunity to approach Sekhmet in her richly appointed
pavilion, red banners flapping, incense smoke curling, plush red
carpets and fresh flowers surrounding her. We approached her
with gratitude, special prayers, and offerings. Typical offerings
were red or black stones such as carnelian, onyx, lava rock; red
flowers, especially roses and poppies; and incense of myrrh,
frankincense, and kyphi. Many brought pomegranate juice as a
libation. The nights were cool in sharp contrast to the days. With
food, song, and prayer aplenty, the devotions lasted until sunrise.

   My last Sekhmet Festival and my last days at the temple

were the culmination of my dreams as a priestess and my desires as a devotee to honor and pay homage in both ancient and modern ways to Sekhmet.

Sunrise

At sunrise on the final day of my last Heart of the Sun ceremony, I placed my ritual Sekhmet necklace over the head of the new priestess, Candace Ross. It was an ending and a beginning for both of us.

EPILOGUE

Ben and I returned to our beautiful home in Oregon's Columbia River Gorge, surrounded by trees, rivers, and mountains. Basking in cool and moist greens, I remembered fondly the hot and dry reds and yellows of the desert.

I resumed teaching and writing. Our schedule returned to a Monday-to-Friday work week. The moon was often masked by clouds and I had to keep looking at the calendar to find the lunar cycle. The stars were hard to locate, visible only in the bit of sky not obscured by clouds and trees. The sun rose and set but I couldn't see the horizon.

I am living now in new cycles. The incredibly long winter nights that begin in late afternoon. The deep silence of the snow. The profusion of daffodils, then tulips, in the spring. The way everything just grows and grows without being tended. The long summer days that start before 5:00 a.m. The absolute ecstasy that everyone feels when the sun shines.

But the desert continues to call me, Sekhmet's fire burning brightly. Every year, I return.

Returning to the Temple

I drive down Highway 95 on the way to the temple. As I pass the last Las Vegas exit, I feel a sense of release. The last housing development, the last chain grocery store, the last dry cleaners, the last McDonald's. It is all behind me. Over a year after leaving the temple, this drive is still familiar. Through the windshield the vista of the desert opens, unfolding like a bolt of cloth, billowing as far as I can see, ending only at the sky. I reach the guest house in the dark and sleep that night, exhausted by travel, filled with a sense of release and a nagging anxiety.

I awaken at dawn; the liquid light spreads over the horizon, unimpeded by buildings and trees. A chill is in the air; autumn is slowly making its presence known. I ponder whether I should have brought so many sleeveless tops. Will it be chillier than I thought? Did I bring all the wrong clothes for my month's retreat?

I find the basket with ritual items in it for use by guests. Matches, check. Incense, check. Names of Sekhmet, check.

I feel anxious. Am I going to experience anything while I'm here? Was it all really a sham? Is there really such a place as sacred land? A temple built to an Egyptian goddess one hour north of Las Vegas—I mean, really. How could that be sacred? Across from an air force base, next to the Nevada Test Site? Wouldn't these things describe the poles of the profane—rampant licentiousness and rampant destruction? Had I just been totally deluded the whole time I was here? Is there really communion with the Divine; is there something sacred that is outside of oneself? The outside that connects with the inside, bringing about communion with the Divine? Can that really happen?

I close the door to the guest house and look up the path, the sun rising behind the temple. I am filled with the power of the rising sun, the birth of the new day. But the temple? Will I feel anything when I'm there? Have I lost whatever I had when I was here as a priestess? And now, I'm wondering if I just made it all up. If it was all self-delusion, self-aggrandizement. If I simply

wanted so badly to feel a connection to something outside of
myself that I was willing to concoct stories of feelings so that I
could feel—what?—less alone?

The path to the temple is short but the day is a little windy.
I amble over the beautiful stone bridge that the new priestess, Candace, and others built after a rainstorm and flash flood
washed out the wooden one. I breathe in the expanse, the view
from horizon to horizon. I follow the dusty trail that I have traveled so many times, gathering the willing twigs for the fire.

Entering the temple, I expect to feel overwhelmed by beauty
and emotion. But instead, I see plastic flowers, and I am overcome with a sense of irritation. One part of my mind goes to my
general dislike of plastic flowers as offerings. Then the other part
of my mind, fueled by my heart, opens. They are offerings, left
here by people who honor the goddesses in the temple. These
are sacred offerings, no matter what my other mind thinks about
them. I sit next to the fire pit, turn off my judgment, open my
heart, and open my eyes to look at Sekhmet.

Gazing up at her, I feel my heart open fully. I see her look
of welcome, her smile. Her gratitude. We are in communion,
together. It is real.

I put the twigs together and light a fire. I sing Sekhmet's
mantra, feeling it suddenly deep in my core. I am filled with
love. I am aware of all the land around the temple that supports
me, that comes to me in love. I feel the immediate response to
my prayers here. Yes, this is what it means to be on sacred land.

Certainly, on some level, all land is sacred. But some land
is more accustomed to being sacred, has built up energy from
all of those who have come to it. And that is what this temple is
like. It holds the thoughts and prayers, the offerings, the pain, the
sadness, and the joy of all those who come here, all those who
surrender themselves to it.

Being here and seeing Sekhmet's radiant smile, knowing that I am now able to receive her smile, I surrender to the ecstasy of the Earth and sing the song of the spirit, here in the embrace of the goddess, at the feet of Sekhmet.

Endnotes

1. For a full account, see Genevieve Vaughan, "My Journey with Sekhmet: Goddess of Power and Change," *SageWoman*, Summer 1998, 42.

2. The Crone is typically a woman past the stage of menopause. She is considered wise and unwilling to put up with foolishness.

3. According to the Ruby Valley Treaty of 1863, the Shoshone have rights to sixty million acres in Nevada, Idaho, Utah, and California, which include Yucca Mountain. The land was never deeded to the United States, though the treaty states that there are certain activities the US can engage in on this land. The US now claims over 80 percent of that land as solely belonging to the federal government due to "encroachment." The federal government has tried to persuade the Shoshone to accept financial compensation for their land, but they refuse. The Shoshone are adamantly opposed to nuclear testing on their native lands. For more information, see www.wsdp.org. For a video about the fight of two Shoshone grandmothers against the federal government for grazing rights, see www.oxfamamerica.org.

4. Vaughan, "My Journey with Sekhmet."

5. "The Book of the Heavenly Cow," translated by Edward F. Wente Jr. in *The Literature of Ancient Egypt*, edited by William Kelly Simpson (New Haven, CT: Yale University Press, 2003); and Normandi Ellis, *Feasts of Light: Celebrations for the Seasons of Life Based on the Egyptian Goddess Mysteries* (Wheaton, IL: Quest Books, 1999).

6. Burning Man, an annual event in Northern Nevada, features "radical self-expression," which includes ecstatic works of art and striking, elaborate costuming.

7. Wicca is a subset of Paganism, often considered to be a modern form of witchcraft. Goddess Spirituality could be considered a subset of Paganism or Wicca, although some practitioners would argue that it is a stand-alone tradition.

8. Kalli Rose crossed over on winter solstice 2009. She is dearly missed.

9. The lyrics to this chant were written by Z. Budapest: "We all come from the Goddess, and to her we shall return, like a drop of rain flowing to the ocean." More about Z. can be found at her website (www.zbudapest.com).

10. *Kyphi* is an Egyptian incense that includes ingredients such as cinnamon, cedar, myrrh, and frankincense.

11. "The Circle Shapes Us" was written by Deirdre Pulgram Arthen.

12. A *dakini* is the female embodiment of enlightenment.

13. For more information on Michael Harner's work, see the Foundation for Shamanic Studies (www.shamanism.org).

14. For more information about Sylvia, see her website (www.sylviabrallier.com).

15. Portions of this section, "Women and the Goddess Temple," appeared on 10/31/2006 in Medusa Coils' blog (www.medusacoils.blogspot.com/2006/10/guest-blog-importance-of-goddess_31.html).

16. Statistics on the religious composition of the U.S. can be found at the Pew Forum on Religion and Public Life (religions.pewforum.org/pdf/affiliations-all-traditions.pdf).

17. Ronald Hutton, *The Religions of the Ancient British Isles* (Oxford: Blackwell, 1993), 337–341.

18. The Tuesday, March 14th, 2006 entry from Herstar Equinox Astrological Report used with permission from the estate of Kalli Rose Halvorson.

19. Katlyn's oils and incenses can be found at her website (www.mermadearts.com).

20. For more on Asherah and the connection with the maypole, see Asphodel P. Long, "The Goddess in Judaism – An Historical Perspective" in *The Absent Mother: Restoring the Goddess to Judaism and Christianity* (London: Mandala-HarperCollins, 1991), 35.

21. Asherah was bred by Serpentessa, a twenty-first-century snake priestess (www.serpentessa.com).

22. See the U.S. Religious Landscape Survey from The Pew Trust poll (religions.pewforum.org/affiliations).

23. Read and listen to "The Water Song" story by Corbin Harney from *Circle of Stones*, a PBS production of indigenous storytellers (www.pbs.org/circleofstories/storytellers/corbin_harney.html). Also see Corbin in the film documentary *Trespassing* or read his book *The Way It Is* (Blue Dolphin Publishing, 1995). Corbin crossed over in July of 2007. He is greatly missed.

24. My thanks to Dr. Candace Kant, who contributed to the invocations and ritual to water, and whose exquisite words continue to grace many temple rituals.

25. Carol Christ, *Rebirth of the Goddess: Finding Meaning in Feminist Spirituality* (New York: Routledge, 2004).

26. The Western Hemisphere Institute for Security Cooperation (WHISC or WHINSEC), formerly the School of the Americas (SOA) is a United States Department of Defense facility that has been widely criticized for training international and especially Latin American soldiers and government officials who have been accused of human rights violations and criminal activity in their home countries.

27. For a picture of the dome in Hiroshima, follow the links to the A-Bomb Dome (www.pcf.city.hiroshima.jp).

28. For reading on Enheduanna, see Betty De Shong Meador, *Inanna, Lady of the Largest Heart: Poems of the Sumerian High Priestess Enheduanna* (Austin, TX: University of Texas Press, 2001). For

reading on Inanna, see Diane Wolkstein and Samuel Noah Kramer, *Inanna, Queen of Heaven and Earth: Her stories and Hymns from Sumer* (New York: Harper & Row, Publishers, Inc., 1983).

29. For readings of these myths, see *The Literature of Ancient Egypt*, edited by William Kelly Simpson (New Haven, CT: Yale University Press, 2003) and Joseph Kaster, *The Wisdom of Ancient Egypt* (New York: Barnes and Noble, 1968).

30. Normandi Ellis, *Feasts of Light: Celebrations for the Seasons of Life Based on the Egyptian Goddess Mysteries* (Wheaton, IL: Quest Books, 1999).

31. Barbara Lesko, *The Great Goddesses of Egypt* (Norman, OK: University of Oklahoma Press, 1999), 145.

32. Ibid.

33. Geraldine Pinch, *Egyptian Mythology: A Guide to the Gods, Goddesses, and Traditions of Ancient Egypt* (New York: Oxford University Press, 2004), 125.

34. Jennifer Pinkowski, "Egypt's Ageless Goddess: A modern pilgrim visits the temple of Mut," *Archeology*, 59, no. 5 (2006), 45–49.

35. Ibid.

36. Jaana Toivari-Viitala, "Women at Deir el-Medina." *A Study of the Status and Roles of the Female Inhabitants at the Workmen's Community during the Ramesside Period* (Leiden: Nederlands Instituut voor Het Nabije Oosten, 2001); and Judy Grahn, *Blood, Bread and Roses: How Menstruation Created the World* (Boston: Beacon Press, 1993).

37. Normandi Ellis, *Awakening Osiris: A New Translation of the Egyptian Book of the Dead* (Grand Rapids, MI: Phanes Press, 1988), 178.

38. Maat is the Egyptian deity of justice; she is the one who weighs the heart of the dead.

39. For more on the Durga Puja, see Laura Amazzone, *Goddess Durga and Sacred Female Power* (Hamilton Books, 2010).

40. Normandi Ellis, *Feasts of Light: Celebrations for the Seasons of Life Based on the Egyptian Goddess Mysteries* (Wheaton, IL: Quest Books, 1999).

41. *Asperges* refers to the act of sprinkling with sacred water. *Aspergers* are those who sprinkle the water.

42. Crone Witch Patricia performed a special ceremony for Willoeh to help her conceive. The lovely Sunflower, Willoeh's daughter, is truly a child of the temple.

ACKNOWLEDGMENTS

My deepest thanks go to all those who have offered help and support throughout the three-year odyssey of this book. This page would not be here without your help. I am especially grateful to my sister, Lori Key. She believed in this book from the very beginning, when it was a jumble of journal pieces glued together with weak transitional sentences. She has read every draft over the three years of writing—always encouraging, always believing, and always willing to read once more.

This book would never have come to its present form without the editorial direction of Sandy Boucher. Her task was to teach an academic writer how to tell a story. Her kind guidance supported the reworking and final shape of this memoir. Thanks also to my copy editor, Arlene Prunkl, who added clarity and consistency to the manuscript.

I am deeply indebted to all those who have read parts of this book through its many drafts. My thanks especially to Candace Kant, Colette Todorov, Delona Campos-Davis, Deb Nervig, Karen Villanueva, Liona Rowan, Joanie Sather, Jen Crum, Dot Hill, Abigail McBride, Deborah La Marcela, Paul Kaspar, Holly Montano, Tom Ascher, Jean Ewald, Laura Snyder, Patricia Monaghan, Mimi Maduro, the Hood River Book Group, Sharon Steele, Rick Hulett, my sister Jamie Ileks, and brother-in-law Ian Flude for their comments and guidance.

Thanks to designer Soujanya Rao, who came to my rescue. Her artistic and clear formatting of this book and the cover design has transformed a text document to a work of art. And my final thanks go to my dear husband, Ben Kuehn. When this book seemed unwritable and my courage flagged, his constant encouragement and support made it possible for me to believe in myself and continue on.

Desert Priestess:
a memoir

A *Goddess Ink*
Reading Group Guide

ABOUT THIS GUIDE

We hope this Reading Group Guide fosters discussion and encourages exploration into the various themes presented in *Desert Priestess: a memoir.* Additional information may be found on our website, www.goddess-ink.com.

Questions for Discussion

1. At the beginning of the book, Anne questions her abilities: "...I felt like a charlatan, an imposter." Have you experienced a similar moment in your life, when you were in a position in which people looked to you for answers, but you felt unqualified to answer them?

2. Anne confronts the need to transform herself: "In the back of my mind, I still saw myself as a college administrator; I could feel the parameters, the box of that profession, as visceral walls. After the first year, I knew that to move ahead, to be effective, I had to step into my power as a priestess, completely and totally." Are there times we need to transform ourselves? How do we know when to let go and what to let go of?

3. In the book, Anne tries to understand the historical Sekhmet and the Sekhmet present at the temple in Nevada. How does history, and historical context, influence myth? Can these myths change, be updated?

4. In the book, Anne describes the people who compose the "circle" of those who attend ceremonies at the temple:

The defining ideal of the circle is the elegant single line, perfectly rounded and seamlessly meeting. As is often the case, the ideal and the reality are sometimes far apart, and the wide variety of people who attended temple rituals didn't always mix well. So instead of one simple elegant line, the reality is that this circle is woven, like a wreath, from local materials that were not cultivated for the purpose of being interwoven. As priestess, I tried to weave these bits of the old and brittle desert-dried twigs with the supple and yellow-flowered creosote branches, the thorny and hardy mesquite boughs and the frayed cotton puffs that blew in from afar. All of these pieces made up our desert wreath, our sacred circle, which in reality was ovoid with bits sticking out on the sides. But it was gritty and real, sublime in its authentic beauty.

What does this say about the perfect images and imperfections of groups? Families?

5. What influence does feminism have on the Goddess Spirituality movement discussed in the book? How do politics and experience influence spirituality?

6. Anne discusses women's and men's relationships to the female Divine. How are they different? The same? Do you see the Divine as female? Why or why not?

7. Has reading this book made you think about religion or spirituality in your own life in a new or different way? How so?

8. What are the spiritual values related in this book?

ABOUT THE AUTHOR

Anne Key was born in Texas in 1963, the eldest of three daughters. She graduated from Stephen F. Austin State University with a BA and MA in English. From 1986 to 1988, she lived in the People's Republic of China and was on the faculty of Hefei University of Technology and Sun Yat Sen University. She relocated to Oregon and began working in administration in the community college system, first at Tillamook Bay Community College and then Columbia Gorge Community College. The locations of these small rural colleges, the Oregon coast and the Columbia River Gorge, afforded her the opportunity to live in a much closer relationship to her natural environment than her previous urban dwelling. Her spiritual seeking in these surroundings brought her to a nature-based spiritual practice.

In 2004, she moved with her husband Ben Kuehn to the Nevada desert, where she was priestess of the Temple of Goddess Spirituality Dedicated to Sekhmet. In one of those rare times in life when the head and the heart meet, in 2005 she completed her PhD in Philosophy and Religion with an emphasis in Women's Spirituality at California Institute of Integral Studies. Her research and dissertation combined her lifelong interest in Mexico and pre-Columbian religion by focusing on female divinities in the Mesoamerican cosmovision. She has also worked as an adjunct faculty member for the College of Southern Nevada in the Women's Studies and Religious Studies departments. In 2007, she and Ben returned to their home in Hood River, Oregon, and with Dr. Candace Kant launched Goddess Ink Ltd., a small press dedicated to fostering and publishing works about the Female Divine.

In 2011, Anne and her husband moved to Albuquerque, NM. She currently resides there with his five cats and her snake, Asherah, a Red-tailed boa. *Desert Priestess: a memoir* is her first full-length book. She is co-editor of *The Heart of the Sun: An Anthology in Exaltation of Sekhmet*, also published by Goddess Ink Ltd. See more of her publications at www.annekey.net and www.goddess-ink.com.

CPSIA information can be obtained at www.ICGtesting.com
Printed in the USA
LVOW061338210911

247247LV00002B/2/P